Myths & Legends of Wales

by Tony Roberts

Illustrated by
Sheila Paton &
Elizabeth Roberts

Published by
Abercastle Publications
Waunblaen, Felinwynt,
Aberteifi, Ceredigion, SA43 1RW
Tel: 01239 811267

Reprinted in
1985, 1986, 1988, 1992, 1996,
1999, 2000, 2008 and 2014

Printed by
Dinefwr Press, Llandybie, Carmarthenshire

Contents

Introduction

This is a selection of some of the most well-known – and some lesser known – Welsh folk-tales, with particular reference to the place where things happened. There is a special fascination for most of us to realise, in a particular village or field or house, that something strange took place a hundred or a thousand years before.

That great scholar, Sir John Rhys believed that folk-tales were not just fairy tales for adults, but were vital and important as part of the history and culture of a nation. He complained somewhat ruefully that Non-conformity and universal education had eliminated belief in the authenticity of folk-tales.

I have tried to give a cross-section of all folk-legends, from the famous traditional tales of the Mabinogion, tales of the Saints, well-lore, cave legends, historical legends, to the beliefs like Phantom funerals and Corpse Candles. What is not so easily apparent in so small a compass is the extent to which these tales were believed in and how closely they touched the life of ordinary people.

This is hardly the place to try and explain the inexplicable; it is enough to say that the historians have not had much success with it. Nowadays they do not even try to give rational explanations but, prudently perhaps, limit themselves to analysing and classifying, tracing international folk-tale elements. So you can accept or reject these tales if you wish – crude superstition? Or was there some strange basis of fact?

Y Tylwyth Teg: The Fair People

The Fairies play such a dominant part in Welsh folk-lore that they seem like a parallel population of the country. All folk-lorists agree how completely people believed in their existence until the rise of popular education.

As well as Y Tylwyth Teg, they were known locally as Bendith y Mamau, the Mother's Blessing, or Dynion Bach Teg, the Little Fair People; and, on the Pembrokeshire Coast, Plant Rhys Ddwfn, the Children of Rhys the Deep (deep meaning cunning).

They were not ghostly. In fact, they were almost human, the women sometimes marrying humans and having children. They lived in communities and were well disposed towards humans. There were some however who were evil-minded and distrustful. There were, in fact, subdivisions of the fairy race.

Often they were tiny, their horses tiny too; their clothes were long and flowing, of fine silk and highly coloured. They lived underground, in caves too, often reached through water, and particularly by or under lakes.

They were also immortal, one account speaking of their living seven years here, seven underground and seven in the air; the reason they were not around after mid-Victorian times was just that they had been exorcised for some generations. Nonconformity and temperance were anathema to them and they left Monmouthshire because there was too much preaching. Their music was wonderful and dancing was one of their principal occupations. They got very cross when grassland, especially that with their circles in, was ploughed up. In fact, they didn't take much to arable farming, and were no good at mending their implements.

Speaking the truth was important to them and they were equally meticulous in leaving money for services rendered, though it sometimes turned into cockleshells or even horse-manure. They had a deep loathing or hatred of iron; they counted in fives, hadn't much of a health service considering how often they used human midwives; they came to wash their children in human farmhouses and left money to pay for it. They had money and treasure and frequented markets, more in west Wales than elsewhere it seems. They didn't like to be recognised in market or street but would willingly draw anyone into their dancing and once there, it was difficult to get out in less than a human year and without the assistance of strong men and a rowan stick or iron.

The Elidorus or Llyn y Fan Fach tales reveal so different a kind of fairy from the 'changeling' or Vengeance stories that it is clear one is reading about differing kinds of Fair Folk. Are they the faint long-remembered memories of an earlier indigenous population (Bronze Age vanquished by Iron) or the souls of the dead awaiting a body and a destination?

Mermaids

People have believed firmly in mermaids all over the world. In some places they still do. Nearer home, the belief was always strong in Celtic countries, the most picturesque accounts generally coming from Scotland. There do not appear to have been any sightings or encounters since the early part of the 19th century, but several specific encounters have never been satisfactorily explained away.

In Wales, mermaid encounters have centred around Pembrokeshire and Caernarvonshire; curiously there are relatively few sightings in Cardigan Bay. In some ways, the mermaids parallel the ladies of the Tylwyth Teg who marry mortals.

Mermaids often had fish-skin caps and were unable to return to the sea without them. They cursed their captors if the latter were unpleasant, and they rewarded them with prophecy if they behaved well.

Giants

There are quite a lot of giants known in Welsh legend, fifty or sixty in all. There is in fact, no particular legend connected with most, but many were killed by Arthur. There were four giants around Dolgellau, the leader being Idris, living in Cader Idris. Then, further north on Aran Benllyn is the grave of Rhitta Fawr, who lived on Snowdon. He was killed in combat with Arthur after having demanded Arthur's beard. On his cloak he had the beards of kings slain by him and he offered Arthur the honour of having his beard placed uppermost, or the alternative was a challenge to fight. Arthur accepted and killed Rhitta.

Three Cardiganshire giants were killed by Arthur's nephew Gwalchmai or, anglicised, Gawain. The job had to be done by cunning, as they couldn't otherwise be killed.

Maelor, another Cardiganshire giant lived near Aberystwyth with his three sons. Captured, he was allowed a final wish to blow his horn three times. The first time his hair and beard fell off; the second time he blew till the nails of his fingers and toes fell off; the third time the horn shattered, but his son heard. As he rode to the rescue his hound's head came off as it couldn't keep up, at Bwlch Safn y Ci (Pass of the hound's mouth). His horse leaped the valley at Ol Carn y March (the Steed's Hoof-mark). But he was killed too. Arthur killed the three sisters of Cribwr, a Glamorgan giant, and he killed several more giants on the Shropshire border who had imprisoned his brother-in-law. Then there are many tales of giants carrying large stones: Merlin reported that giants had moved the Stonehenge stones 'from Ireland'.

Giants were also addicted to throwing large boulders and taking huge leaps.

There are a number of legends of stones being carried by giants, and of giant leaps and Arthur stones too. There are stupid giants, child-eating giants.

There is no real guide to the date of the giants, though if one were taking them literally they could be placed in some cases to Arthur's time. But they do seem to reflect some telescoped time-scale with which an older civilisation is mistily recalled.

Evil Spirits, Witches and Wizards

Folk-tales about the Devil are mostly confrontations in which the Evil One is frustrated. Witch tales are very widespread reflecting an almost universal belief in their existence but those about Wizards are nowadays less known. In Victorian times and earlier there was a special class of man called a Dyn Hysbys, variously translated as Wizard, Conjurer, Wise Man, all seemingly somewhat inadequate.

Witches existed in most communities and were feared and shunned and of course mercilessly persecuted in earlier times. They could put a curse on people or livestock, and could change themselves into cats or hares. A witch's spell could be broken in a number of ways: the intervention of a priest, reading the Bible over the person or animal bewitched, keeping a Bible in the house, using a ring of mountain ash, or rowan, nailing up a horse-shoe, drawing blood from the bewitched animal, sprinkling the earth from a church-yard, or using the power of a Wise Man.

Some Wise Men had sold themselves to the devil but the more normal type was one who used his powers for the good; these powers he obtained from books or had inherited. There were a large number of these men and it was usually quite easy to consult them and pay a small sum for a charm or remedy to cure an ailment, human or animal.

Evil spirits, then as now, tended to have a religious connotation. Many of them got into churches and had to be exorcised or sometimes literally dragged out.

Historical Legends

The earliest historical anecdote is that of St. Peter clearing Heaven of a crowd of garrulous Welshmen by going outside the gates and shouting 'Toasted Cheese' (Caws Pob) whereon all the Welshmen rushed out. Several of the most entertaining ones come from Giraldus Cambrensis, Gerald de Barri or Gerald the Welsh-man, the 12th ecclesiastic who fought vigorously against King and Canterbury.

His early and moving statement of Welsh nationalism is that of the old man of Pencader. King Henry II on a punitive expedition in south Wales asked a faithful old supporter what he thought would be the outcome of yet another rebellion. The old man replied, ". . . this nation, O King, may be harassed, weakened and destroyed by you and other powers, though it can never be totally subdued by any man unless God shall concur. Nor do I think that any nation than this of Wales, nor any language, shall answer for this corner of the earth."

King Arthur

King Arthur was a great Celtic hero, a military leader against the English or Saxons. He appears regularly in the Welsh folk-tales, as a fighter pure and simple, for the Round Table and Grail elements of the stories were French additions later on. But since the whole of Britain was Celtic at this time, he appears in the folk-tales of many parts of England too.

In Wales, he appears in the very earliest tales of the Mabinogion and again in the latest, where the tinge of medieval romanticism has overlain the folk element. Most interestingly, his name is perpetuated topographically in numerous places; and in the story of Culhwch and Olwen, the battle between Arthur and the Twrch Trwyth can be followed across Pembrokeshire and onwards, place by place.

Although Arthur appears in the histories of the time, such as they are, he is a folk-lore figure in a world of magic. He fights giants, is worsted by a Saint, seeks the cauldron of the King of the Otherworld, hunts the boar and disinters the head of Bran, buried in London. Fascinating stuff, but to include them all would need a much larger book.

The Saints

In the fifth century, Saintship was already a profession in Wales, especially in the West and North. The Saints were, in many cases itinerant monks coming from princely families. They sailed round the dangerous and rocky West and North coasts and founded their tiny cells, living simply and preaching their austere gospel.

Nothing was recorded of their activities for hundreds of years, and when their biographies were written, the credulity of medieval religiosity revealed some strange things.

Heads were cut off, picked up and put back. Among others St. Winifred, St. Justinian, St. Cynog and St. Decumen suffered in this way. St. Piran sailed from Ireland on a sea monster, St. Feock on a granite boulder, and St. Decumen, as well as his headless accomplishment, sailed on a bundle of twigs.

St. Brendan, riding from Ireland on a sea monster met St. Barre riding the opposite way on a horse.

The austere St. David confined his miracles on the whole to occurrences of a religious nature – healing his teacher Paulinus's blindness, or raising a hill at Llandewi Brevi on which to preach against Pelagianism.

At times, saintliness got mixed up with the fairies and their magic world: St. Collen has a successful set-to with Gwyn ap Nudd, King of the fairies, and one version of the Llynclys lake story is that the inundation of the wicked king's palace was due to his refusal to listen to St. Garmon's sermon against Pelagianism

Among the Saint stories are several dealing with serpents: St. Carannog even tamed and fed a huge harmless serpent. But St. Samson gave off such an odour of sanctity that a serpent, unable to bear it, ate itself up, starting at the tail. St. Kenedlon, daughter of Brychan founder of the Kingdom of Brecon, came to a wood after crossing the Severn, and when she prayed, all the serpents in it were turned into stones.

Sunken Lands

From North to south Wales there are stories of Sunken Lands. The most famous is the Cantre'r Gwaelod, a fertile territory extending from Pembrokeshire to Bardsey Island covering all Cardigan Bay. Then, in Conway Bay, there was Llys Helig; and in Caernarvon Bay, Caer Arianrhod though this was little more than a single stone. In the South, the Glamorgan Coast from Mumbles to the River Ogmore was inundated in the same way as Llys Helig.

Among the lakes of Wales, many have sunken cities: Llyn Safaddon in Breconshire, Llynclys Lake near Oswestry, Llyn Tegid (Bala), Crumlyn near Swansea, and Llyn Llion. Many of the inundation tales were stories of retribution against wicked kings.

The Cantre'r Gwaelod tale is very similar to that of Lyonesse off Cornwall which had cities and 140 churches, and where King Arthur and his Knights had many adventures; Tristram was even born there. According to the Anglo-Saxon Chronicle, Lyonesse was destroyed in the 11th century.

There is a strong basis of fact behind the Sunken Land tales but there is no geological evidence that inundations took place in historical times and the Stone Age period is, according to Dr. North, more likely. The long stone walls beneath the sea in Cardigan Bay are more probably glacial moraines.

Dogs of the Otherworld (Cwn Annwn)

The Dogs of the Otherworld were a pack of small hounds headed by a large dog; their howl was terrible to listen to and foretold death. At their approach other dogs stopped barking and fled in terror. Birds stopped singing and everything was hushed. They howled particularly at crossroads and collected in church-yards, disappearing at the place where the person whose death they foretold was to be buried.

It was said that the nearer they were, the less their howling sounded.

Their colour was given as white with red ears.

The Mabinogion

The most famous Welsh folk-tales of all are called The Mabinogion and were translated by Lady Charlotte Guest about 1840. They had existed in written form in Welsh since the 14th Century but they had been told for centuries before that, by the professional story-tellers. It does not need much imagination even today to picture how these strange tales would have sounded before smoky wood-fires in medieval hall or castle. How far back the oldest go, is guess-work, but there are echoes of a forgotten mythology and of the early Celtic pagan gods.

The first four stories are called the Four Branches and tell of the lives and deaths of early Welsh kings and mythical figures. Although this is a world of magic, it is firmly rooted in the soil, set in places that exist today, mainly in Caernarvonshire and Pembrokeshire (or perhaps we should say Gwynedd and Dyfed).

The Four Branches are entitled:

Pwyll, Prince of Dyfed
Branwen, daughter of Llyr
Manawyddan, son of Llyr
Math, son of Mathonwy

Five of the other seven stories are about King Arthur and his knights in, again, a similar land of enchantment, filled with giants and fabulous beasts. The most fascinating tale, possibly the earliest, is Culhwch and Olwen. This is the story of Culhwch's quest to win the beautiful Olwen, daughter of the fearful Chief-giant Uspaddaden. He is helped by Arthur, the knights and magical companions in the battle against the monstrous boar Twrch Trwyth with a comb and scissors in his head.

The Dream of Rhonabwy, Peredur, The Lady of the Fountain and Geraint all have a different air about them. The heroic age of chivalry is coming and while there is fantasy, there is less crude vigour than in Culhwch; more romance and less hacking off of giants' heads.

Two stories standing apart are The Dream of Macsen and Lludd and Llevelys, the latter about King Lludd of Britain and the former about the Roman Emperor Magnus Maximus who was closely associated with Wales – his 'chair', Cadair Macsen, stands on the top of the Freni Fawr in the Preseli Montains and his wife Helen, a Welsh Princess, has given her name to Sarn Helen, an important early highway.

The Story of Pwyll, Prince of Dyfed

Pwyll went hunting from his chief palace at Narberth to Glyn Cuch. Losing his companions, he came across a stag hunted down by strange dogs glistening white with red ears and eyes. He drove them off and set his own dogs on, when up came a stranger clad in gray, on a gray horse. He reproved Pwyll, who handsomely apologised. The stranger was Arawn, King of Annwn, the Celtic Otherworld. Pwyll agreed to do him a favour which was to spend a year in Annwn, looking like Arawn and living like him, and to kill his enemy Havgan. This had to be accomplished with only one stroke, for, with more, he would recover. In return Arawn would rule Dyfed for a year. All this took place, and Dyfed prospered.

Then Pwyll courted the fair Rhiannon; it was difficult at first since her white horse, though walking slowly, could not be overtaken at the fastest gallop. But at last, by the simple expedient of speaking to her, she stopped. At their betrothal feast though, Pwyll was asked a boon by Gwawl, which he thoughtlessly granted; Gwal asked for Rhiannon, whom Pwyll then had to give up, a year hence. But Rhiannon, after telling Pwyll off, got over this by producing a magic bag which Gwawl was induced to get into. It was then tied up, and Gwawl got a beating ... "and then was the game of Badger in the Bag first played."

Then the nobles of Dyfed came to Pwyll at Preselau and grumbled that he had no heir, and wanted him to take another wife. Pwyll asked for another year, and a little boy was born. But he disappeared the night he was born. Rhiannon's servants, afraid they would be blamed and killed for this, blamed her and charged her with devouring the child. Rhiannon had to do penance.

The little boy suddenly appeared in the house of Teirnyon, Lord of Gwent Iscoed, who had a fine mare which foaled on the 1st May always; unfortunately the foal always disappeared. One night, she was brought into the house to foal so Teirnyon could watch; when the mare foaled, a huge claw came through the window to take the colt. Teirnyon cut off the claw with his sword and dashed out in the direction of the noise and

wailing that followed. He found nothing but when he came back, there was a baby boy. Eventually he heard about Rhiannon's trouble, and recognised the boy as Pwyll's son. So he took the child back.

The boy was called Pryderi and he ruled Dyfed after Pwyll.

This is a very muddled story, full of loose ends in the form we have it today.

The Second Branch: Branwen daughter of Llyr

Matholwch, King of Ireland, arrived at Harlech to ask for Branwen, daughter of Llyr, in marriage. This was arranged with her brothers, Bran and Manawyddan, and they were married at Aberffraw. Their bad-tempered half-brother Efnisien mutiliated the Irish horses and the insult was with difficulty appeased by the present of a magic cauldron and much compensation.

The Irish returned home and later, after the birth of a son Gwern, Branwen was unjustly humiliated and punished by the Irish. After a message reached him, Bran invaded Ireland. Irish treachery was foiled by Efnisien, who killed secretly hidden Irish warriors concealed in sacks ostensibly full of flour. But he later threw the boy into the fire and the Irish fought back. Their cauldron of rebirth which healed their dead was broken by Efnisien who died in breaking it.

Although victorious in the battle there were only seven British (Welsh) left. Bran is mortally wounded and at his own request his head was cut off, to be taken to the White Mount in London. Branwen died of grief; the survivors spent seven years in Harlech feasting, and the three birds of Rhiannon came and sang sweetly to them. They then spent eighty years in Gwales, which is perhaps Cemaes in Pembrokeshire or perhaps Grassholm Isle, 'in a fair and regal spot overlooking the ocean'. Then they opened a forbidden door and had to continue their journey to London to bury the head, after its sojourn of eighty years.

The Third Branch: Manawyddan son of Llyr

Pryderi gave his mother Rhiannon in marriage to his friend Manawyddan, after the sad journey to London with the severed head: "in her prime," he said "none was ever fairer. Even now she is not uncomely," he added, rather ungenerously.

But after they had hunted and feasted, the whole of Dyfed through a strange enchantment became desolate with heavy mist, the houses emptied, people disappeared. So they went to England to earn their living. Manawyddan was so excellent a saddle-maker, shield-maker and cobbler that the English wanted to kill them; so they returned.

Pryderi and Rhiannon became magically stuck to a golden bowl on a marble slab in a castle which then vanished in a mist. The capable, cautious Manawyddan again went to work and then, bringing seed back from England, sowed grain, farmed and hunted again in Narberth. When he came to harvest, hordes of mice ate the wheat on the stalk; but he captured one of the mice and proceeded to hang it as a thief.

Passers-by tried to stop him, and it turned out the mouse was pregnant and the wife of Llwyd of Kilcoed who had enchanted Dyfed in revenge for the insult inflicted on Gwawl by Rhiannon and Pwyll. So, in return for the life of the mouse the enchantment was lifted and Dyfed prospered.

The Fourth Branch: Math son of Mathonwy

Math, Lord of Gwynedd, had to live with his feet in a maiden's lap, except when at war. Goewin the maiden was desired by Gilvaethwy, so his brother Gwydion, a cunning magician, made a plan to obtain her. They went to Rhuddlan Teifi in Ceredigion, he exchanged the precious swine which Pryderi had been given from the Otherworld, for horses and dogs which were magic and later disappeared.

So, Pryderi, angry at being deceived, made war on them; and Gilfaethwy ravished Gowein. But by magic and deceit, the men of Gwynydd won, Pryderi was killed. Math punished the criminal by changing them into animals.

Arianrhod, Math's niece, was proposed as a new foot-holder but she failed to pass the test as a maiden, and had a fine fair-haired baby, then called Dylan, Son of the Wave. There was another boy, whom Arianrhod swore never to name; neither could he ever bear arms or have a mortal wife. Gwydion brought the boy up and, by cunning, circumvented all Arianhod's conditions: first, naming him Llew Llaw Gyffes, then getting arms brought by subterfuge to Castell Arianrhod, then getting Math to help making a maiden out of broom, meadowsweet and oak blossoms called Blodeuwedd and she became his bride. She took a lover, Gronw and they plotted to kill Llew Llaw Gyffes who could be killed only on Sun-

days, not within a house or without, neither on horseback or on foot and only by a wound from a spear a year in the making.

Llew was changed by the wound into an eagle. Gwydion found and restored him, Gronw was killed and Blodeuwedd changed into an owl, the enemy of all other birds.

Other tales of the Mabinogion

The three other tales, Peredur, Geraint and The Lady of the Fountain are much influenced by the medieval French romantic tradition, though they are thought to have originated in south-east Wales unlike the Four Branches, which are specifically centred round Pembrokeshire and Caernarvon. The three romances are set in King Arthur's court but the landscape is, unlike the familiar one of the Four Branches which is dotted with well-known place names, a vague and romantic one, and the action full of medieval knight-errantry. It is in fact hard for the scholars to know whether these stories came originally from Wales or from France.

Then there is the story of Lludd and Llefelys which tells of the three afflictions of Britain – the Coroniaid, a people who could hear and know everything said in the land; a terrible scream heard every May eve which left men faint and women and animals barren, and finally a giant who made everyone sleep and took away all food and drink. Llevelys saves Lludd's kingdom: the Coranians he got rid of by talking through a huge brass horn and then poisoning their water with insects. The scream he diagnosed as coming from two dragons fighting, and they were made drunk with mead and then buried. The giant was defeated in combat by Lludd.

The Dream of Maxen Wledig centres round the historical Roman Emperor Maximus, elected Emperor by his soldiers in Britain in 383 A.D. and who took the Romans away from Britain and was killed by Theodosius in Europe five years later. The heroine is Helen, a Welsh princess.

Macsen, in a dream, falls in love with the princess and then, awake, tries in vain to find her. Finally, he re-enacts the wanderings of his dream, goes hunting, crosses the sea and eventually comes to Caernarvon where he finds the princess and marries her. There is a lot of detail: how the roads through Wales were called after Helen Luyddawc, Helen of the Legions, how Caernarvon, Caerleon and Carmarthen castles were built for her and how Maxen, going hunting one morning, set his chair on the top of the Freni Fawr in Pembrokeshire in the spot today called Cadair Macsen.

There is another dream story, *The Dream of Rhonabwy*, Arthurian, a rather satirical tale, with a jumbled and inconsequential story. Characters pop in and out, Arthur plays a long game of chess, armies fight, ravens attack: a parody almost of the traditional tale.

Culhwch and Olwen was probably the earliest tale and it brings in so many interesting events out of the gamut of the international folk tale. The hero sets out to marry the giant's daughter and has to fulfil a series of quests. It is a long and muddled tale: lots of the tasks are forgotten, but those that are followed up are fascinating and the intervention of Arthur and his extraordinary men – no courtly knights here – and the hunting of the monstrous boar, the humour and the ebullience make much of the Four Branches seem lack-lustre. Here it is – Culhwch was the son of a prince and, though he had never seen her, he fell in love with Olwen, daughter of the savage giant, Yspaddaden Penkawr.

"Go to Arthur your cousin," said his father, "and ask him to cut your hair and help you."

Arthur cheerfully offered the assistance of all his knights and they set out to achieve the seemingly impossible tasks set by the giant, at which everyone hitherto had failed.

They had to grub up a hill, plough, sow and ripen the grain in a day, find the missing Mabon lost in infancy, hunt the Twrch Trwyth and perform numerous other tasks, and if successful, the giant would die.

Mabon was found by asking the oldest creatures, blackbird, stag, eagle, owl and salmon, the other tasks accomplished by magical help and the hunt for Twrch Trwyth begins.

The mysterious Twrch Trwyth was a monstrous boar, with seven young pigs, transformed for his sins from a King into a swine. Between his ears he had a comb, razor and scissors which Arthur had to take as one of the impossible tasks.

So Arthur went to Ireland to ask for the comb etc., but the Twrch was so angry at being transformed to a swine that he wouldn't speak to Arthur, let alone yield comb, razor and scissors. What was more, he took the battle into Arthur's country. With his seven young pigs, he landed at Porth Clais. Arthur and his men, horses and dogs went to Mynyw (St. David's), missing Twrch whom he overtook after the pigs had killed all they found of men and beasts along Abergleddyf (Milford Haven).

Arthur followed Twrch Trwyth as far as Preselau and Twrch made a stand along the Nevern. From there he went to Cwm Cerwyn and slew four of Arthur's champions; and made a second stand and slew four more, and was wounded himself. The next morning before day, he killed four more and, with these, many men of the country.

Then Arthur pursued him to around Llandissilio and he killed four more before going on up to Cardiganshire; all over south Wales they chased the boar and pigs, losing many men. Eventually only Twrch himself was left and in the Severn estuary, they seized the scissors and razor but he escaped to Cornwall where they managed to get the comb. But Twrch swam out to sea and was seen no more.

Culhwch and Arthur's men went to the giant and cut off his head and Olwen became Culhwch's wife.

Gazetteer of Folk-Tales

HOLYWELL (Treffynnon) Flintshire

Holywell takes its name from the holy well of St. Gwenfrewi or Winifred. She was a niece of St. Beuno, and the daughter of Thenith a local ruler who had appointed Beuno as her religious instructor in return for a piece of land for a church.

Caradog, the son of a local chieftain Alyn from Penarleg (Hawarden) 'endeavoured to force her chastity', but, having taken her vows, she resisted, and fled to St. Beuno's church. Caradog chased her and when she still repulsed him, drew his sword and cut off her head. A healing well gushed forth where the head fell. Her head rolled gently down the hill to the church. The congregation, surprised to see the head roll in went outside, to find the murderer wiping his sword 'on the grasse'. Beuno picked up the head and cursed the young man who died on the spot and

disappeared from sight. The saint then joined the head to the body, covering it with his mantle, and returned to the church to say Mass, and prayed. The girl rose up 'as if from sleep', with a white circle, as small as a thread, round her neck. She spent the rest of her life as a nun, becoming Abbess at Gwytherin in Denbighshire.

Bueno cursed Caradog's descendants who barked like dogs and could be cured only by immersion in the well.

In 1138 Winifred's relics were enshrined in the Benedictine abbey church in Shrewsbury.

King Henry VII's mother, Lady Margaret Beaufort had the well enclosed in a stone building and it continued to be a centre of pilgrimage even under the Reformation. Daniel Defoe noted in the 18th century that priests were in disguise, and in 1719 the authorities sent dragoons to seize the priest as he was officiating. By the end of the 18th century there were, according to the traveller Thomas Pennant, every species of frolic and excess among those who had gathered there 'for unseemly ends.'

LLYS HELYG

A great tract of country was once supposed to have existed from the Great Orme to Bangor and from Llanfairfechan to Ynys Seiriol or Priestholm. The court stood halfway between Penmaenmawr and Great Orme

Head. A calamity had been foretold four generations before it came and it was a vengeance on Helig ap Glannog for his wickedness and impiety. As he rode through his fertile acres one day, a voice warned him that "Vengeance is coming." He asked when and was told that it would come in the time of children of his great-great grandchildren. He reflected that it wouldn't at least come in his lifetime.

When the time did come, and the family were taking part in the festivities, a servant going to the cellar to draw more mead, noticed that water was forcing its way in. He had time only to warn the King's harper before the inundation. As with Llynclys, Llyn Safaddon, and Llyn Tegid, it is always the harper who gets away.

There is a variation of the Tyno Helig story which says that Helig repented and became a monk.

LLANDRILLO, Denbighshire

Two men were otter hunting in Cwm Pennant, Llandrillo, when they saw something reddish scampering across the ground in front of them. They thought it was an otter and they watched it and saw it enter a hole beside the river. When they got there, they found two holes in the ground below the tree roots. So they pushed a long stick into one and in the normal way held a sack across the mouth of the other. After a while, their prey scuttled out into the sack which they picked up and carried back home.

They had not gone far when they heard a little voice say "My mother is calling me." They were so startled they dropped the sack immediately. A little man in red crawled out and promptly ran away as fast as he could to the river bank.

Similar stories come from several other places in North Wales.

RUTHIN, Denbighshire

A Fairy Cow has been reported in many places but the most well-known, Y Fuwch Frech, the Freckled Cow, lived on a farm Cefn Bannog (after the mountain ridge of that name), a few miles from Ruthin. Whenever anyone needed milk they went to this cow with a vessel and however big the vessel, they always went away with it filled. This continued until one day a witch went and milked and milked the cow until she was dry, after which the cow went away, and was never seen again.

Tradition says that she went to a lake a few miles away, followed by her children the two long-horned oxen, to Llyn Dau Ychain, lake of the Two Oxen, and, bellowing, all three disappeared beneath the water.

But there is another tale about the Two Oxen. In those days, a wicked spirit troubled Cerrig-y-Druidion church and everybody was very much afraid to go near the church and see the evil one looking out grinning at them. A wise man told them the only way to get rid of the evil one was to use the Two Long-horned Oxen, which grazed up on Waun Bannog. They yoked the oxen and with difficulty got the spirit on to a sledge to which the oxen were yoked.

LLANGOLLEN, Denbighshire

The town is named from St. Collen, a wandering saint of the 6th century, honoured also in Cornwall. He was of 'illustrious ancestry' and fought as a soldier against Julian the Apostate, returned to Britain, and retired to a cell on a mountainside.

One day he heard two men talking about Gwyn ap Nudd, saying he was king of the Tylwyth Teg and Lord of the Unknown. Collen told them to shut up, as Gwyn and his men were devils. That night, there was a knock on the door and a messenger said he was from Gwyn ap Nudd, who was inviting Collen to meet him. Collen did not go; the messenger came again and still he did not go. A third time the messenger came, and said this time it would be the worse for Collen if he didn't go.

The next day, Collen went, taking a pitcher of Holy Water. He saw a fine castle, wonderfully dressed ladies and men with attendants, and he was courteously taken to the king for dinner. The king welcomed Collen and hoped he would stay some time.

"I will not eat the leaves of the forest," replied Collen.

"Did you ever see men better dressed than my attendants?" asked the king.

"They are well enough dressed," said Collen, "considering what dress it is."

"What kind of dress is it?" asked the king.

"The red on one side indicates burning, and the blue on the other means freezing," answered Collen, and he flung his sprinkler of holy water in the faces of the king and his people. The whole scene disappeared, castle, king, men and women.

VALLE CRUCIS ABBEY, Llangollen

Two miles from Llangollen is Valle Crucis Abbey, or rather the ruins of what was one of the finest Cistercian monasteries of medieval Wales. Unlike the Benedictines who stayed close to their Norman masters, the Cistercians or White monks adapted well to Wales, especially to the lonely parts and the upland moors where they had enormous flocks of sheep.

It was the Abbot of Valle Crucis, out walking one morning early in the hills near the Abbey, who met Owain Glyndwr, last great fighter for the independence of his country. Glyndwr greeted the Abbot and remarked on his early rising. "No," replied the Abbot, "It is you who have risen too early, my lord, a hundred years before your time."

This remark refers to the coming of the Tudor dynasty which was, perhaps mistakenly, seen by many Welshmen as the fulfilment of prophecies about the liberation of their country.

LLANEILIAN, Denbighshire

St. Eilian was a Welsh saint of the 6th century and a well flowed in response to his prayers; at least that was the official story; from what pre-Christian source it was taken over, is not known. Up to the 18th century it was an ordinary healing well, but then it changed and became feared for its evil powers. For it had become a cursing well and it was widely believed that a person cursed there could die.

For the cursing, a frog was impaled on a skewer and a cork put on both ends. It was then floated and the cursed person would suffer while the frog remained alive. Or names were put in: a three by two inch piece of slate was found in the well, initials scratched on, a wax figure pinned through the centre.

At Llanllawer in north Pembrokeshire, bent pins were put in the well for cursing, straight pins for blessing.

Ffynnon Elian was certainly the most notorious evil well. Its owner in the early 19th century made a good income from those cursing and those wanting to be relieved from the curse.

At one time, an old woman used to enter victims' names in a book and threw a pin in the well in the victim's name; and for a fee she would take it out. The well was emptied before she began the cursing ritual. Various passages of the Bible were used in connection with both cursing and lifting rituals, the Psalms and the Book of Job being felt the most appropriate in the lifting. The celebrated Jac Ffynnon Elian, the best known 'priest', who was jailed several times for cursing people, used a copy of the Apocrypha in the ritual.

Despite the magistrates' opposition, it took many years before the belief in the cursing disappeared (if it has); now the well is covered up.

HU GADARN – *HU THE MIGHTY AND THE AFANC IN THE CONWAY*

Hu Gadarn is described in the ancient Triads as 'he who first taught the

Cymry how to plough land' when they were in Gwlad yr Haf (the land of summer) and led them to the isle of Britain. He would not take territory by force but only by justice and in peace. His were the famous horned oxen with which he dragged the Afanc from Llyn Llion to prevent an inundation.

But the more well-known tale about two long-horned oxen (Dau Ychain Banawg) is that of the River Conway Afanc. At Llyn yr Afanc on the Conway, a girl enticed the Afanc out of the water. While he slept with his head on her knees, and one claw-like hand on her breast, he was bound by chains. When he awoke in a fury, he made for the pool, throwing everyone aside. His hand tore the girl's breast off, and back to the lake he went, leaving the chain on the bank.

The famous oxen were sent for and the chain fastened to them. They dragged him out and up to Llyn Cwm Ffynnon Las where he was left. They went through the pass Bwlch Rhiw'r Ychain where one of the oxen dropped an eye (Gwaun Llygad Ych and Pwll Llygad Ych).

There is a similar tale about Llyn Barfog, but here King Arthur and his war-horse dragged the Afanc out. But about this lake, there is a more famous legend which is on page 25.

BODFARI, Denbighshire

Dr. Edward Williams, a well-known clergyman, wrote in his autobiography about an incident that had remained with him all his life. It was in the early eighteenth century when, as a child, he was playing with companions in a field called Cae Caled near their house.

Suddenly they saw seven or eight couples dancing less than a hundred yards away in the middle of the field. It was midsummer, a little after noon. The people were dressed in red, without hats, their heads tied with red handkerchiefs spotted with yellow. In their hands they held white handkerchiefs held loose. They were about the same size as the children, but adult.

The children, frightened, made for the stile. There were no soldiers anywhere near, it was not the time for May dancers and moreover these people were unlike any the children had seen. Then one of the dancers turned and ran after the children. Dr. Williams, the youngest, was last and as he ran for the stile and climbed over, saw behind him 'the ancient, swarthy and grim complexion' of his follower reaching out to seize him.

LLANLLECHID, near Bangor, Caernarvonshire

It was at one time intended to build the church of Llanllechid in a field called Cae'r Capel not far from Plas Uchaf farm. The day after starting, though, all the materials had been taken to the place where the church now is, and first day's work had been destroyed.

The workmen took all the materials back and started again. But again, the following day, the same thing happened. The workmen realised they were fighting against a superior power and it was useless to continue. So they built where the present church now is.

There are similar legends about the churches: Corwen, Capel Garmon, Llanfair, Dyffryn and Clwyd. In the last one, the removal was attributed to a phantom in the shape of a sow's head. The farmhouse subsequently built on the site is called Llanbenwch – the church of Sow's Head. There is a similar legend about a church in Lancashire at Winwick.

At Llanfihangel Geneu'r Glyn, it was intended to build the church where a farmhouse, Glanfread Fawr, stands now. Each night the portion built during the day was pulled down. At last, a spirit spoke saying:

> Llanfihangel Geneu'r Glyn
> Glanfread Fawr shall stand herein.

At Wrexham a spirit called out "Bryn y Grog" and the church was then built at Bryn y Grog hill.

NANT Y BETWS, near Caernarvon

One moonlight night, the son of Ystrad farm went to Lake Cwellyn and hid, to watch the Tylwyth Teg dancing. He saw a beautiful girl whom he fell in love with.

On a sudden impulse, he leaped into the ring, seized the girl and made off with her. He got her home and treated her so well that she agreed to be a farm servant. She did her work wonderfully well especially the milking; the cows seemed to give twice as much for her. One thing she would not do, and that was to give her name.

Then quite accidentally one night driving a couple of cows to their grazing, the young man came to the place he had captured the fairy girl. He hid and overheard two fairies saying "When we were last here, our sister Penelope was stolen by a man." He went home and called her by her name, which greatly surprised and upset her.

He asked her to marry him; at first she wouldn't, but later agreed with one condition: that he should never strike her with iron. If he did, she would leave him for ever. He readily agreed and they lived happily for many years. They had a family and prospered. Then one day, they went out to a field to catch a horse which was untamed and while they were at work, he rashly threw the bridle over the horse while the wife was close by, and the iron touched her. She immediately disappeared and was never heard from again – except on one cold wintry night when she came to his bedroom window and told him to take care of the children.

It is from this family that a family called Pelling, well-known in those parts, descended.

This tale might be called the prototype of many legends, especially in north Wales, of human-fairy marriages. Nearly all follow the same pattern except that the hiding of a fairy's name is an element of the international folk-tale that has somehow found its way in.

PENMYNYDD, Anglesey

There was an old legend many centuries ago, that a great poisonous serpent living near-by would kill the heir of Penhesgyn.

Then, one day, a clever young man thought of a way of getting rid of it. He dug a hole and put a large brass pan in it so that when the serpent looked at it, a reflection looked back. Thinking it was another serpent, he attacked it and when he was exhausted fighting his own reflection, the man killed him.

The threat removed, the heir came home and a celebration took place. Then the heir wanted to see the serpent's body, so it was dug up for him to see. He kicked idly at the dead serpent and, as he did so, a fang entered his foot and he died. Thus the old legend came true.

ANGLESEY: LEGENDS OF THE DRUIDS

There is so much legend and so little fact about the Druids that historians have found it hard to distinguish one from the other.

The Druids officiated at the worship of the Gods, regulated public and private sacrifices and ruled on all religious questions. They were held in great honour and instructed the young men in their art. They were judges and adjudicated in disputes. The Druid doctrine was strongest in Britain and those in Gaul who wanted to make a profound study went to Britain for it. The immortality of the soul was the foundation of their philosophy. They were the learned priestly class among the Celts.

A foremost Druidical college was on Môn (Anglesey) and this was destroyed with great bloodshed by the Romans under Suetonius Paulinus in 61 A.D.

" ... a dense array of armed warriors and between the ranks ran women in black with dishevelled hair waving torches. All round, the Druids lifted their hands to heaven and scared the Romans by uttering dreadful imprecations," so Tacitus said.

And Caesar added that: "wickerwork images were made and filled with living men and then set on fire." The gods apparently preferred the execution of criminals, but the deficit was made up by the innocent.

We shall probably never know if the Druids possessed the principles, unknown to us, of divining the centres of energy. Other ancient writers praised their learning, wisdom and search for a sublime truth. Anglesey was the area associated with the Druids, but practically nothing is known of them or their rites now.

LLANGWYFAN, Anglesey

On the south side of Mynydd y Cnwc in Llangwyfan parish in south-west Anglesey is Arthur's Cave. At high water, the cave mouth is covered by the sea, but the large cave has a vent-hole in the mountainside. The cave contains various treasures left by King Arthur in the course of his war with the Irish who had then invaded parts of Wales and temporarily conquered them. There was also on top a cromlech around which was a circle of stones and beneath which was treasure, an ancient chest full of gold. The supernatural guardians of the treasure have prevented anyone from digging it up.

LLANDDONA, Anglesey

The notorious witches of Llanddona, and their husbands, came by boat, having been expelled from their original country. When their rudderless and oarless boat first approached the shore, the local Welsh people tried to drive them away again and even after they had landed, they were not allowed to leave the beach.

The strangers, although exhausted from hunger and thirst, commanded a spring of pure water to appear from the sands.

Then they were allowed to stay, but they were universally feared and disliked. The men lived by smuggling and the women by begging and cursing. The witching power was thought to descend from mother to daughter; they visited farmhouses and with their dishevelled hair and bared breast demanded charity which none dared refuse. Such was the fear of them that when they went to market to buy a pig, people would not bid against them because they could bewitch the animal.

THE COW OF LLYN BARFOG, Merioneth

A variation of the Fairy Cow legend is that of the stray cow of Llyn Barfog belonging to the Gwragedd Annwn, the Ladies of the Otherworld. They would occasionally visit the upper world, clad in green robes, accompanied by their milk-white cattle and white dogs, the Cŵn Annwn.

An old farmer at Dyssyrnant became the lucky captor of one of their cattle and added the cow to his own herd. He became famous and successful because of the abundance and richness of the milk and butter, and the many fine calves. Then fearing the cow was getting old he fattened her for the butcher. The day for the slaughter arrived, the butcher was about to kill the animal, when there came a cry from the heights above Llyn Barfog and one of the ladies in green stood there calling her cattle. The cow and all her progeny, to the third and fourth generation, followed her up the hillside and when the panting farmer himself followed, all he could see was the lady and cattle descending into the lake.

ARENNIG, Merionethshire

In the western end of the Arennig Fawr is a cave; in fact there are several, some very large, but there is one which had the reputation of being inhabited by the Tylwyth Teg. In mid-Victorian times, the local shepherds were enchanted by one remarkable young lady called Mary. They often tried to catch her or even meet her face to face but she was too quick for them. They used to see her though, day after day, with her little harp, climbing the bare slopes of the mountain. And in warm misty weather the beautiful music she made was carried on the breeze.

MOEL EILIAN, Nant y Betws, Caernarvon

Between Llanberis and Cwellyn, the Tylwyth Teg of Nant y Betws lived. They were said to live in caves in the mountains and if anyone could find the entrance of their cave, he would find a considerable amount of wealth, because they were very accomplished thieves.

They went to fairs and stole from farmers; they lurked around people's houses and took butter and cheese from the dairies and if they could do so unobserved, milked the cows and goats. And they carried away unbaptised infants.

But there was another kind of Fairy very unlike the former. These latter were far more beautiful, honest and good towards mortals. It was they who were seen on moonlight nights singing and dancing, or sometimes hunting on their grey horses. Though they were said to be immortal, they ate and drank like human beings and married and had children. They were very clean and neat and used to reward clean servants and hospitable farmers' wives.

So it was for them that bread and washing water were left overnight. This kind of Tylwyth were said to live underground and the way to their country was under hollow banks, overhanging lakes or deep river pools. When they came out in daylight, one could stop and chat with them. These were the fairies men fell in love with.

It was dangerous to go near their ring when they were dancing because they would draw a man in and bewitch him and make him invisible to his companions (many people used to go and watch the fairies), and he would

be detained as long as he lived, unless he could be got out before cock-crow. The way to get him out was by handing him a long stick of mountain ash when his turn in the dancing came and pull him out.

BEDDGELERT, Caernarvon

The most famous legend of the locality is the one about Prince Llewelyn and his hound. In the 13th Century, Prince Llewelyn the Great lived at his palace and often used to go out hunting. One day Gelert, the leader of his pack of hounds, did not come immediately when he called, so he left the dog behind.

When he returned after hunting, the dog came out to greet him, but to his horror he saw the dog's jaws dripping with blood. With a terrible premonition, he dashed in to see if his child was safe, following a trail of blood to the baby's room. He found a scene of disorder and an overturned cradle but no child to be seen.

Mad with grief and rage, he drew his sword and killed the dog. Then, behind the overturned cradle, he saw the baby lying unharmed; and beside him lay the dead body of an enormous wolf.

Grief-stricken, Llewelyn, carried the body of the dog outside and buried him; a cairn of stones marks the spot. This tale is an 18th century fabrication, invented it is said, by the landlord of the Goat Hotel.

Also about Beddgelert, a different type of tale is about the man who sat down to watch a large gathering of fairies. He fell asleep and the fairies came and bound him with ropes of gossamer, covering him so that he could not be seen. For a whole day his family searched for him without success. The next evening the Fairies returned and released him.

DINAS EMRYS, Vortigern and Merlin

A few miles north of Beddgelert is the site of the fortress of Dinas Emrys, and we move back to the 6th century A.D. when Vortigern, King of Britain, 'oppressed by his enemies', invited Hengist and Horsa to help him. He married Rowena, Hengist's daughter, in exchange for Kent. But once the Saxon savages were in, they treacherously slaughtered Vortigern's nobles.

His wise men advised him to build a fortress and retreat to it. So they went to Eryri (Snowdon), assembled workmen and started to build. But the foundation they built by day, subsided by night. Vortigern was told to find a fatherless youth, sacrifice him and sprinkle the blood on the stones and in the cement.

Messengers were sent out and eventually came to Carmarthen, where they found Merlin, whose mother was daughter of the King of Demetia, but had no father. They were sent to Vortigern where Merlin's mother was respectfully received but Merlin was upset on being told his blood was needed for a sacrifice.

Merlin told Vortigern to have his men dig below the foundation and they would find a pool. This was confirmed and Merlin asked the wise men what was beneath that. They did not know.

"Drain the pool," said Merlin, "and you'll find two sleeping dragons."

This too was done and Merlin was proved right. Two dragons, one red and one white, came out from inside two stones and started to fight. At first the white had the better of it and put the red to flight, but later the red fought back and expelled the white.

"I shall now unfold the mystery," said Merlin. "The white dragon is the Saxon and the Red is the British; the pool is a symbol of the world. At first the invader will triumph, but the Welsh will one day be free again."

There were many prophecies made by Merlin, some of great national portent, some trivial.

About his death there has always been mystery. In Brittany he is supposed to sleep in the Forest of Broceliande behind an impenetrable hedge, his head on the knees of Viviane. He may also be in a cave in Bryn Myrddin (Merlin's Hill) near Carmarthen; another account has him in an unpleasant hollow cave under a rock among the woody hills of Dynevor. According to the Triads, he went to sea in a house of glass taking with him the 13 curiosities of Britain including The Veil of Arthur which made the wearer invisible, the Horn of Brangalad which provided any liquor desired, Rhydderch's dish on which any meat desired would appear; a golden chessboard with men of silver who would play themselves; and a knife which was used for Druidical sacrifices. In his dome of glass, according to the story, he lies on Bardsey. There is also an Arthurian story about Dinas Emrys.

DINAS EMRYS AND BWLCH Y SAETHAU

Arthur and his men set out from Dinas Emrys to cross Hafod y Borth mountain for a place above the upper reach of Cwmllan called Tregalan where their enemy were. They pushed the enemy up the pass towards Cwm Dili. But as the vanguard reached the top a shower of arrows came over and killed Arthur.

Arthur fell there and his body was buried in the pass so that no enemy should pass that way. A heap of stones there today is called Carnedd Arthur, Arthur's Cairn; and the pass, Bwlch y Saethau, the Pass of the Arrows.

Then after his death, his men descended to the ridge of Lliwedd and down from there to a vast cave called Llanciau Eryri, the Young Men of Snowdon's cave. This is in Cwm Dyli and there they are still sleeping waiting in their armour for the second coming of Arthur to restore the crown of Britain to the Cymry.

As the local shepherds were one day collecting their sheep on the Lliwedd, one sheep fell and a shepherd climbing after it, found himself by the hidden cave of Llanciau Eryri. He looked in and saw the warriors. As he was squeezing in, he touched the bell and the warriors awoke with a terrible shout, terrifying the shepherd.

The cairn on the top of Snowdon which existed till it was demolished and the hotel built was called Carnedd y Cawr, the Giant's Cairn, and there was buried the Giant Ricca, or Rhitta.

DOLGELLAU, Merionethshire

A villager was returning from Dolgellau to Llanegryn across the mountain one evening at dusk when he heard close to Lake Gwernen a voice crying out from the water, "The hour is come but the man is not."

As he went on his way he came across an insane looking man wearing nothing but his shirt. The man was rushing full pelt into the lake.

There was a similar story about Lake Cynnwch to the effect that on the eve of New Year's Day a man was seen going back and forth shouting out the same sentence. This seems to suggest the survival of an ancient lake sacrifice story.

ABERDARON, LLEYN, Caernarvonshire

A farmer living at Deunant near Aberdaron, used to go out of his house a few steps every night to relieve himself before going to bed. But one night while he stood there, a stranger was standing beside him.

"You have no idea," said the stranger, "how annoying this is for me and my family."

"But how can that be?" said the farmer.

"My house is directly below," said the stranger. "Just stand on my foot and you will see what I mean."

The farmer did so, and he could see how all his slops went straight down the other's chimney which stood far below in a road he had never seen before.

The fairy then suggested he had a door made in the other side of the house and that if he did so, his cattle would never suffer from anthrax. The farmer did this and he became the most prosperous stock rearer in the area.

LLANFROTHEN, Merionethshire

A man fell in love with a beautiful Tylwyth lady and wanted to marry her. She consented but warned him that she would leave him if he ever touched her with iron. He accepted the condition but thought little of it. They were married and lived happily for many years and had several children. But an accident happened to them one day. They were crossing Traethmawr at Penrhyndeudraeth on horseback together when the man's horse became restive and jerked his head towards the wife and the bit of the bridle by accident touched her left arm. She told her husband that she must leave him straight away. He was terribly upset and implored her not to. She said she could not stay.

Then he appealed to her for the children and begged that she would stay for them. What, he said, would happen to them without their mother.

Her strange answer was:

"Gadewch iddynt fod yn bennau cochion a thrawynau hirion." Let them be redheaded and longnosed.

Then she disappeared and was never seen again. But there was in fact a type of Welshman with these characteristics, redhaired and longnosed. The Wild Men of Mawddwy were like this. The Wild Red Men began their outlawry in the 11th century, but Tacitus mentions redhaired Britons, so it is difficult to date their appearance.

DINAS DINLLE, Caernarvon

Caer Arianrhod was the home of Arianrhod in the Mabinogion; it is now to be seen from Dinas Dinlle as a rock near the shore. There are a number of tales about it; mainly they concern three beautiful sisters and that while they were away, the castle was inundated.

DEGANNWY, Merioneth

The Creuddyn Peninsula, especially the rock of Degannwy, was the favourite place of the great 6th century King of North Wales, Maelgwn Gwynnedd. His advent to power was the result of competition. He and his rival princes sat in their chairs on the sands in the Dovey estuary. The incoming tide routed his competitors, but Maelgwn had provided himself with a floating chair.

Powerful though Maelgwn was, and Gildas (the 6th Century Saint and historian) grudgingly pays tribute to him in his contemporary history, he could not escape the Yellow Plague which devastated Europe in the middle of the 6th century. "And Maelgwn Gwynnedd beheld the Yellow Plague through the keyhole in the church door and forthwith died." One account of the Yellow Plague is as a strange beast with yellow eyes, teeth and hair; and another describes it as a column of vapour rising from earth to heaven and sweeping along the ground. The church where he died was thought to be Eglwys Rhos, not far from his court.

PENRHYNDEUDRAETH, Merionethshire

A young woman left a house in Penrhyndeudraeth one night to return home, accompanied by her family's manservant, David Williams, known, because of his size and strength, as Dafydd Fawr, Big David. It was a dark, calm night, Dafydd, carrying a flitch of bacon on his back was walking a little behind his young mistress. She went straight home, thinking he was following.

But three hours went by before he arrived. Asked about it, he said he was only three minutes after her. When he was finally convinced, he accounted for the long delay in the following way.

He saw a brilliant meteor flying through the air, followed by a hoop of fire, in which stood a handsomely dressed, though small, man and woman. They had one arm round each other, the other holding on to the hoop, and their feet braced on the inside rim. As it landed, they jumped down and made a circle on the ground. A number of other men and women appeared and they all began dancing round, to the loveliest music Dafydd had heard.

He stayed, as he thought, a few minutes to watch. The ground was lit up by a subdued light and he could watch everything. Then the meteor returned with the hoop and the first two people jumped in again and took off and the others disappeared and Dafydd continued on his way.

SWYDD FFYNNON, Cardiganshire

An interesting tale of a midwife was told by Pali Evans who died a hundred years ago. She had been called to attend a confinement and found everything in splendid order for it was a very grand house and the lady was the wife of one of the princes. But Pali could see nothing but the lady and the baby. Everything was done noiselessly and Pali saw nobody else. She was given ointment to rub the baby with after bathing it morning and night, and she was warned not to put any near her eyes. One day her eye happened to itch and she rubbed it, she saw everything much more clearly. Small men and woman were going quietly about, preparing food and looking after the lady carefully, the house and furniture were luxurious. Pali said to her, "You have had a great many visitors today." "How do you know," said the lady, "You have put the ointment into your eyes." And straightaway she got out of bed and blew into Pali's eyes, and said, "Now you will see no more." From then on, she never saw the fairies again. Nor was the ointment entrusted to her again. According to a slightly similar version, the midwife went to Ffair Rhos between Ystrad Meurig and Pontrhydfendigaid. There she saw a great many of the Tylwyth including the lady she had attended. When she went up and greeted her, the lady spat in her face, and she never managed to see the fairies again.

CASTELLMARCH, near Abersoch, Lleyn

Ond of Arthur's warriors was March Amheirchion, lord of Castellmarch in Lleyn; and, like King Midas, had horse's ears. He kept his hair long and to prevent anyone knowing his secret, he killed every barber who came to shave him and cut his hair.

On the spot where he used to bury the bodies, reeds grew and when one of these was cut to make a pipe, it played no other sound than: 'March Amheirchion has horse's ears'. When March heard this he would probably have killed the innocent player on the spot, except that even he himself, could not make the pipe play another tune.

So he gave up the pretence and had his hair cut normally.

This tale is interesting in that it dates back to a time when a pipe, not the harp, was the favourite musical instrument. And there was an ancient Irish King with horse's ears.

ST. BEUNO at Clynnog, Caernarvonshire

When St. Beuno lived at Clynnog, he used to preach regularly at Llanddwyn. Walking along the shore one day, he dropped his book of sermons and it was swept away by the tide.

He looked for it everywhere and finally found it again, with a curlew standing beside it keeping guard. Beuno fell to his knees and asked the Lord to bless the curlew and the Lord granted the blessing of making the curlew's nest very hard to find.

BORTH: CORS FOCHNO, Cardiganshire

Cors Fochno is a large bog inland from Borth and at one time it was inhabited by a terrible witch, called Yr Hen Wrach. She was seven feet tall, thin and yellowish with a huge head covered with jet black hair. Despite all the precautions they took, the witch got into houses and blew a sickness into people's faces, causing an ague-like illness.

LLANARTH, Cardiganshire

A mermaid often used to be seen on a rock known as Carreg Ina near New Quay. One day she was entangled in the nets of some fishermen who were a good distance out. She asked them to disentangle her and put her back in the water. They did and she warned them of a coming storm. This story is also told of Aberporth and is similar to the tale of the St. Dogmael's mermaid.

THE WILD RED MEN OF MAWDDWY, Merionethshire

The best known legend of the days of robber bands comes from that most beautiful and wild landscape of the Mawddwy valley.

One famous band which defied the law after the establishment of the Council of the Marches at Ludlow were the Gwilltion Cochion Mawddwy, the Wild Red Men of Mawddwy.

On Christmas Eve 1554 the great robber clan were gathered together feasting and celebrating in the Pass of Fedwen when Baron Owen, Sherriff of Merioneth, made a strong attack with a large force and succeeded in surprising and capturing eighty of the gang.

As Christmas Day dawned, he had them hanged from the branches of trees there. While he watched a woman dashed forward and, baring her bosom, cried: "These breasts have suckled those you are murdering and those who will wash their hands in your blood."

A year later, when he and his retinue were coming from Welshpool, a barrier of trees halted them, and a shower of arrows shot from an ambush surprised them. The Baron was dragged from his horse and cut to pieces at a place known today as Baron's Gate.

CANTRE'R GWAELOD, Cardiganshire

The Cantre'r Gwaelod, or Bottom Hundred, was a great tract of fertile country extending from Ramsey Island north to Bardsey Island over what is now Cardigan Bay. It was 40 miles long and 20 wide, low and level, highly populated and cultivated, with 16 fortified towns 'better than all the towns of the Cymry except Caerleon-on-Usk'. The King was called Lord of Cantre'r Gwaelod in Dyfed, although most of the land lay closest to what is now Cardiganshire. It was defended from the sea by a strong embankment and sluices.

The Lord of the Cantre'r Gwaelod in 520 A.D. was Gwyddno Garanhir; and the Keeper of the Embankment was Seithennin, 'one of the three immortal drunkards of Britain.'

One evening there was a great banquet and Seithennin, in his usual state, left the sluices open. The sea came in remorselessly and the land was inundated. Those of the inhabitants who were not drowned escaped to Ardudwy, part of Caernarvon, and ascended the mountains of Snowdonia, the first time they had been populated.

Nowadays when the sea is very still and the water clear, the walls and buildings are said to be seen still, and when the water below moves them, the church bells sound faintly.

LLANYCHAEARN, ABERYSTWYTH, Cardiganshire

In July 1826, a farmer in Llanychaearn whose farmhouse was 100 yards from the sea, went down to the cliff and within a stone's throw from him, saw a beautiful girl washing herself. At first he turned away then realised that it was high water and must be fully six feet deep. So he lay down on the cliff and watched her for half an hour. Then he went back to get his family. Since it was only six o'clock they weren't all dressed. But they went down, the farmer's wife and younger child last. The farmer's wife did not creep along but walked upright and the mermaid saw her and swam out some way. The whole family, including men and maid-servants, twelve in number, watched for half an hour. Sometimes she was swimming, sometimes out of the water to her waist on a rock. She was, the family said, like a young woman of 18, with dark, short hair, unblemished breast and white skin. She bent down frequently as if drinking, and when she did, a black thing like a tail was to be seen behind her. She often made a noise like sneezing.

CENARTH, Cardiganshire

One calm hot day when the hay was being got in, a woman left her year-old baby in his cradle she went into the fields for a while. A neighbour, an old woman of eighty, called out to her that her baby was crying so she went back and comforted the child. But to her surprise, the baby had an old look about him and the neighbours all agreed that he was one of Rhys Ddwfn's children. So they sent for a Wise Man as fast as a horse could bring him. He said he could manage to get her baby back. A shovel was made red-hot in the fire and held before the child's face. In an instant the little being took to his heels and neither he nor his like was ever seen after. And the mother found her own child at the same time. (The children of Rhys the Deep was a local Pembrokeshire name for the fairies.)

ABERYSTWYTH: DEVIL'S BRIDGE, Cardiganshire

The Bridge built by the Devil is the lowest of three built close together over the River Mynach below Bryn Garv where the gorge is deep.

An old woman's cow became stranded on the far side and the Devil offered to build her a bridge there if she would give him the first living thing to cross. When she agreed he built the bridge, thinking she would be the first being to come over after her cow. But she outwitted him by throwing a piece of bread across and her little dog dashed over ahead of her.

MOEDDIN, Cardiganshire

At Moeddin was recorded one of the most impressive phantom funerals. It was observed by a farmer and his wife one evening when they were out working, making sheaves out of the reaped corn after a dry day in a wet summer.

There was a bright harvest moon. Suddenly, while they were working, they heard voices; the parish road incidentally passed alongside their field. Then there came into view a great procession, followed by a coffin on a bier. So great was the crush that some walkers came on to the cornfield. But the farmer and his wife, strain as they could, were unable to make out any words. Uneasily, they went home, leaving the corn. Further along the road, the procession met a tailor, pushing him out of the way on to the verge of the field.

Three weeks later, the real funeral came past this way.

Incidentally, Moeddin was a centre for fairy activity too. But while phantom funerals were seen by those with second sight, there is no record that the ability to see the Tylwyth Teg was also so restricted.

LLANIESTIN, LLEYN, Caernarvonshire

A farmer's wife who lived at the Nant in Llaniestin parish was frequently visited by a fairy who used to borrow her 'padell a gradell' (the wooden shovel used in cooking bread) and repay her with a loaf, carried on her head. One day the fairy came to borrow her wheel for spinning flax. When she handed it over, the farmer's wife asked the fairy's name as she came so often, but the fairy refused to tell her. But as she watched her spinning, the fairy sang to the whirl of the wheel:

Bychan a wydda' hi	Little did she know
Mai Sili go Dwt	That Sili go Dwt
Yw f'enw i.	Is my name.

A Corwrion fairy sang much the same ditty when she came out of the water to spin.

DENNANT, Montgomery

Out hunting one day. Brochwel, a 6th Century Prince of Powys, came across a strange young woman. She was sheltering an exhausted hare which his hounds had chased through the forest. He realised that she was a holy person and gave her land on which to build a chapel.

She was named Melangell, and as Saint Melangell she became the patron saint of hares.

THE GREEN ISLES OF THE SEA, Pembrokeshire

A century ago, so the tradition says, sailors on the coast of Pembrokeshire had actually landed on islands out at sea where the Plant Rhys Ddwfn, Children of Rhys the Deep, lived. This was the name given in west Wales to the Fair Folk. The curious thing was that when the sailors returned to their boats, the islands simply vanished from view.

But the Fair Folk were-well known: they used to come to local markets regularly at Haverfordwest, Milford, Laugharne, Cardigan and Fishguard. They were seen sometimes by a few sharp-sighted people, but their presence was known by many.

"Oh, they were here today," people used to say to each other on their way back from market when prices had been high and everything sold. Without speaking they bought their meat, corn and other necessities, putting down silver pennies as if knowing what they would have been charged. The farmers liked them because they bought corn well, but the poorer labourers resented their forcing up prices.

Gruffydd ab Einon was in St. David's churchyard one day when he suddenly saw the islands out at sea. He went to put out to sea at once but the islands had disappeared; a second time, too, the same thing occurred. The third time, though, he took with him the turf on which he had been standing, and he landed on the islands safely. He was warmly welcomed by the little people and shown their many treasures, for they were great traders.

"How do you manage to stay here in safety?" he asked one shrewd little old man, before leaving.

"There are strange herbs that grow here and nowhere else, so that the islands cannot be seen. Only here do they grow and on the turf in St. David's churchyard; and also on one square yard on one place in Cemaes."

"But how can you be sure that one of you won't betray the secret of the herbs?" persisted Gruffydd.

"Oh," said the little man, "that is due to the teaching of Rhys, patriarch of our people. He told us to honour our parents and ancestors; to love our wives without looking at those of our neighbours and to do our best for our children. We do that, and no-one is unfaithful to another. A traitor is a wholly imaginary character among us: we see him with a head like the Devil, and ass's feet, and hands like a man's, holding a large knife and the family dead around him."

Gruffydd continued to be a friend of the children of Rhys and became very wealthy, but after his death, relations between the Rhysians and farmers in Cardigan became strained because the farmers put the prices too high and the Rhysians took offence. The old people thought they then went to Fishguard as very strange people had been seen there, and it was, after all, before the days of tourists.

THE BOY ON THE FRENI, Pembrokeshire

One day, a boy of about twelve or so was looking after his father's sheep on the Freni Fach, not far from Crymych. The scene then must have been a little different from what it is nowadays – less fencing and no forestry, but the little Welsh mountain sheep in the clear June sunshine looked much the same. And there is now a metalled road round the foot of the Freni Fawr, the bigger hill, under a mile away. These hills are great stretches of moorland and pasture at the eastern end of the Preseli mountains.

When he got to the pasture, there was still a little mist on the mountain top and he looked over to the Freni Fawr to see which way the mist was going. The people in those parts always said that if the mist went down on the Pembrokeshire side, the weather would be fine, but if it went down on the Cardigan side, it would be bad.

As he looked round the still and tranquil scene, he suddenly started with surprise, for over on the Freni Fawr was a party of what looked like soldiers, busily occupied. "No," he said to himself, since he knew the ways of the military, "Soldiers wouldn't be out so early in the day. Anyway, they're too small for soldiers." So he walked further up the hillside and to his surprise, they really were Tylwyth Teg or the Fair Folk; and they were dancing.

He knew all about them of course, everyone did, and he had often seen their rings, but he had never seen them before. He thought of running

home to tell his parents, but decided against it because there was every chance the fairies would be gone by the time he got back.

So he decided to go nearer to get a better view, and anyway he didn't think the Little People would hurt him. He edged nearer and soon he was unobtrusively stationed quite close to the ring, and he stayed there some time watching. As he described them later, they were of both sexes, extremely handsome and very cheerful. They were not all dancing, but those who did stayed carefully to the circle. Some of the ladies were riding on small white horses. All were elegantly dressed in different colours – it was the red coats which had made him think at first they were soldiers.

After a while they saw him and made signs for him to join in; and as he put one foot in the ring, he heard the most beautiful and irresistible music. Almost immediately he found himself somehow in an elegant palace. Here he was liberally entertained, accompanied by beautiful girls, and offered mouth-watering foods, instead of the usual 'tatws a llaeth' (potatoes and buttermilk), and wine in abundance brought in golden glasses. One restriction only was laid on him: he was not under any circumstances, to drink from a well in the middle of the garden. He solemnly agreed not to, and the round of pleasure went on.

Then, one day, an innate curiosity got the better of him, and he plunged his hand in the forbidden well. The fishes instantly disappeared, a confused shriek rang through the hall and garden. Instantly the palace disappeared and he found himself back on the hillside and the sheep peacefully grazing as he had left them (sheep unlike cows are not responsive to the Little People).

Sadly he looked round the hillside for any signs of the Little People or the ring or castle. But, of course, there were none.

THE WATER HORSE OF ST. BRIDE'S BAY, Pembrokeshire

The Ceffyl Dŵr, or Water Horse, was one of the most firmly believed spectres in rural Wales in the past. It was generally a small but beautiful horse which tempted unwary travellers to ride but suddenly galloped away throwing the rider to destruction, except ministers who were allowed a peaceful journey.

The Water Horse was often seen on the shore, dappled, grey or like the sand in colour. One was seen in St. Bride's Bay after a storm. A farmer caught it and harnessed it to the plough. Everything went well for some weeks. Then, apparently seized with an impulse, the Water Horse dragged both plough and ploughman through the field at a furious pace, down to the shore and into the sea, disappearing in the waves.

THE TOADS OF TRELLYFFANT, Pembrokeshire

A curious story is told of the farm called Trellyffant near Nevern. If you go on the coast road from Newport to Moylegrove for about 4 miles, the farm lies down to the right and there is a fine prehistoric burial chamber in a field just visible from the road.

But the story, as told by Giraldus Cambrensis, relates how a young man, Cecil Longlegs, "during a severe illness, suffered as violent a persecution from toads, as if the reptiles of the whole province had come to him by agreement; and though destroyed by his nurses and friends, they increased again on all sides in infinite numbers; being wearied out, he was drawn up in a kind of bag into a high tree, stripped of its leaves; nor was he there secure from his venomous enemies, for they crept up the tree in great numbers, and consumed him to the very bones."

CILGERRAN: THE BEAVERS OF THE TEIFI, Pembrokeshire

The river on which Cilgerran stands is the Teifi, justly famous for its salmon, the finest in Wales, as Giraldus Cambrensis said even before 1200. But in Giraldus's day there were also beavers on the Teifi, the only river in England and Wales still to have them. Giraldus pays tribute to the skill of beavers building their fortifications in the middle of rivers with the "appearance of a grove of willow trees, wide and natural without, but artfully constructed within."

But, continues Giraldus, without a hint of irony, "when the beaver finds that he cannot save himself from the pursuit of the dogs that follow him, that he may ransom his body by the sacrifice of a part, he throws away that which by natural instinct he knows to be the object sought for, and, in the sight of the hunter, castrates himself; and if by chance dogs should chase an animal which had previously been castrated he has the sagacity to run to an elevated spot, and there lifting up his leg, shows the hunter that the object of his pursuit is gone And to corroborate his account of natural history, Giraldus quotes Juvenal and St. Bernard.

YSTRAD MEURIG, Cardiganshire

Between the Teifi and Ystwyth basins, near Ystrad Meurig, many people had seen the Tylwyth Teg; a local blacksmith said they were all ladies in knee-length dresses; but most accounts say they were all beautifully dressed in long elegant dresses, but in varying colours.

FISHGUARD 1797, Pembrokeshire

On 22nd February 1797, an unseasonably hot Wednesday, a retired sailor, John Williams, who farmed Treleddyn, St. David's, watched four men-of-war passing St. David's Head. Though they wore British colours, he recognised them as French. Sounding the alarm, he followed them on the coast.

The ships entered Fishguard Bay at 2 p.m. The fort at Pen Parc fired – though they had only three rounds – and the ships tacked back round Pencaer, anchored and landed troops and stores at Carreg Gwastad, an exceedingly difficult task up a steep cliff. But it was accomplished by the early hours of Thursday, and the Second Black Legion, some 1400 Grenadiers and military convicts under an elderly American, Tate (who spoke no French), was ready to start the career of terror and destruction laid down in their orders.

The first thing they did was to loot the farms on Pencaer, eat ravenously, calves, sheep and poultry, 'geese boiled in butter', and get so drunk on brandy and wine that many were ill for weeks. Pickets were posted at Garn Gelli and Garnwnda.

There was no body of professional soldiers to oppose them. Colonel Knox marched the Fishguard Militia in the direction of Haverfordwest as fast as he could, hastening past the side roads lest he be seen by the French. On the way he met the troops raised by Cawdor coming the other way.

The Lord Lieutenant, Lord Milford, had promptly handed over command to Squire Campbell of Stackpole, newly created Lord Cawdor, who had studied military tactics, but who had never heard a shot fired in anger. He mustered some 500 assorted men to oppose the French and stationed them on the hill before Goodwick Sands. The country people with home-made weapons and some 400 Welsh women with their red cloaks and tall hats crowded the hills too.

The frigates sailed away at noon on Thursday, and Tate with his drunken troops was left to advance on the British. The bad shape of the Legion was emphasised by their threatening to shoot their officers in response to an order of Tate's to punish one man.

By 10 p.m. on Thursday, the French force offered to capitulate without firing a shot, and on Friday this was confirmed. The Invasion was over.

The news of the surrender spread: "It was a grand sight," said an eye-witness, "to look on the surrounding hills crowded with unnumerable spectators of both sexes; the women, in their scarlet mantles and round hats, appeared at a distance like so many soldiers."

At 2 o'clock on Friday, the Frenchmen, drums beating and colours flying, laid down their arms on Goodwick Sands, crying: "To the devil with the Republic," and flinging down their tricolour cockades when Lord Cawdor told them to think no more of the Government that had abandoned them.

The Invasion was over but the legend of the Welsh women lived on, and in particular that of Jemima Nicholas, "a tall stout Amazon masculine woman who worked as a cobbler in Fishguard. Imbued with the noble and patriotic spirit of the old Cambria, she took a pitch-fork and boldly marched to Pencaer to meet the invading foe. On her approach she saw in a field about twelve Frenchmen. Not a whit daunted she advanced to them and whether alarmed by her courage or persuaded by her rhetoric, she had the address to conduct them to the guard-house at Fishguard."

The authorities, in their panic, arrested two Dissenters, but there was nothing they could be found guilty of, even by a panicky Tory Government.

A WITCH AT WALTON WEST, Pembrokeshire

A well-known old witch was coming home from Haverfordwest fair one day in a cart with a farmer who had kindly taken her. As they were driving along the road between Haverfordwest and Walton West, they saw three teams harrowing in a field.

"Could you stop those teams by spells?" asked the farmer.

"I could stop two of them," said the witch, "but the third team master has a piece of mountain ash fast to his whip so I cannot do anything to him."

THE MERMAID AT ABERBACH, Pembrokeshire

It was in the early part of last century when, one fine morning early, the farmer at Treseissyllt went down to the sea at Aberbach. Aberbach is a small and lovely beach at the end of a tiny, and now, wild valley. It has a fine big shingle bank thrown up at the mouth of the valley; and sand and rocks at low water. The cliffs on either side are wild and dangerous, especially on the north where the large farm of Treseissyllt, large for north Pembrokeshire that is, extends to the cliff edge.

It was low water and as the farmer came down to where the lime kiln is, he stopped suddenly. For, stranded inside the shingle bank by the retreating tide, was a young and beautiful mermaid. Mermaids are always described as beautiful; and this one really was, we are told. Perhaps it is only the rather vain and beautiful ones who spent so much time by the shore and on the rocks doing their hair, who got caught by retreating tides.

Anyway, without more ado, the farmer picked her up, thrashing about wildly, and carried her up the path to the farm where he put her in a tub, which he filled with salt water. She pleaded tearfully for him to let her go, but he only chuckled.

"Oh, no, " he said, "I've got other ideas for you." At this, she became really afraid. Finally, in a rage, she put a curse on the farm that no child would be born there again; and then the farmer, rather alarmed, did take her back again and put her in the sea.

For over, a hundred years, the curse hung over the heads of the farmers of Treseissyllt.

An yet … there was some compensation. "Duw, duw," said one old farmer, who was leaving, to his successor, "You're a lucky man."

"Why?" asked the younger man, surprised

"Well, you won't be able to get the servant girls into trouble, will you?"

THE ST. DOGMAEL'S MERMAID, Pembrokeshire

One fine September afternoon at the beginning of the eighteenth century, a fisherman from St. Dogmael's named Pergrin, or Peregrine, was fishing near Cemaes Head. Thinking he saw some movement, he went

silently inshore towards a recess in the cliffs, and there on a rock, he saw a mermaid combing her hair. Quietly but carefully he came alongside and, jumping out, seized her and carried her back on board, struggling wildly and threshing about with her tail. But Peregrine had got her securely and she could not get away.

We do not know what language mermaids speak normally, but this one spoke fluent Welsh and between her tears she begged Peregrine to let her go. But it is not every day that one finds a mermaid and he was most reluctant, although he was rather distressed to see how upset she was. Then, with a last effort, she said, "Peregrine, if you will let me go, I will give three shouts to you in your hour of greatest need." So Peregrine released her, thinking he would never really see her again. And for weeks he did not. Then one hot afternoon, when the sea was calm and Peregrine and a number of other fishermen were out fishing, he suddenly saw the head and shoulders of the mermaid appear in the sea by his boat.

"Peregrine, Peregrine, Peregrine," she cried urgently, "Take up your nets, Take up your nets".

Peregrine was surprised for the afternoon was fine, and the sea showed no sign of any danger. But he instantly pulled in his nets with haste and back he went, past the bar and no sooner was he in than a terrible storm broke out. Eighteen others who had gone out were all drowned.

SAMSON IN NORTH PEMBROKESHIRE

A mysterious series of Samson monuments exists in north Pembrokeshire. At Longhouse farm near Abercastle the famous cromlech is called Carreg Samson; Trellys cromlech in St. Nicholas is Ffyst Samson (Samson's Flail). On the Islet off Abercastle is the Grave of Samson's Finger, though it is marked as natural on the O.S. map. It is incidentally directly aligned with Carreg Samson on the mainland as you climb up the island and look back through Cwm Badau.

In Nevern there is a Bedd Samson (Samson's Grave) and in Llanfyrnach is a great stone said to have been thrown from the summit of Freni Fawr in the Preselies. On the Pencaer peninsula, not far from Abercastle and St. Nicholas are two more cromlechs also called Carreg Samson, at Garn Wen and at Garn Wnda. Stone Age burial chambers antedate St. Samson, however remote he may seem to us, by some three thousand years. We shall probably never know by what process Samson's name came to be associated with them; if indeed it is the same Samson, as the 6th century abbot of Caldy and Dol in Brittany.

ST. BRYNACH IN NORTH PEMBROKESHIRE

A widely travelled 6th century Irishman with noble connections, Brynach, came to Milford Haven where a nobleman's daughter fell in love with him and gave him a love potion. He resisted the 'assaults of fornication', but the angry young lady sent some thugs after him and beat him up.

Brynach went up to the Gwaun Valley and freed Pontfaen from the evil spirits that had made it uninhabitable with their 'horrid howlings'. But he could not settle there and so he went on up the valley and finally to Nevern where an angel told him to look for a white sow who would show him where to build his church; and this he did.

Like St. David, his contemporary, Brynach lived austerely, wearing rough clothes, helping the poor and living a life of constant fasting and prayer. Wild beasts became tame for him; two stags drew his cart, his milk cow was looked after by a tame wolf, and he communed with angels on the top of Carn Ingli behind Newport.

THE VISION AT MORFIL in the Preseli Hills, Pembrokeshire

In 1853 Mr. John Meyler of Cilciffeth was walking home from Morfil one night. The prehistoric Flemings Way crosses the present day B4313 here; on the left looms Mynydd Cilciffeth and to the right, as you come from Morvil are the Preseli Hills proper, Foel Eryr first. Even nowadays, all round are lonely, brooding expanses of moorland.

When Mr. Meyler neared Penterwin, about a third of his way home he saw the image of armies in the sky. There were several battalions at first, but then they increased till they went right across the sky. There were two opposing forces discernible and he could distinctly see men falling and horses galloping across the heavens.

He was so terrified that he called at Penbanc and Mr. James Morris, who lived there, went out and saw the same thing. The whole phenomenon lasted about two hours.

A PHANTOM FUNERAL in the Gwaun Valley, Pembrokeshire

Together with the Corpse Candle, the Toili or Phantom Funeral was the most prominent death portent in Pembrokeshire. This Gwaun Valley story dates from this century.

A young man who worked as a porter on the G.W.R. near Cardiff came home ill. A friend of his sat up with him all night. About three in the morning, the friend was so worried that he went for the patient's father, an elderly man living in a cottage near by.

As he went outside, he found, to his astonishment, that he was in a large crowd of people, and there was a coffin resting on some chairs, ready to be placed on the bier. The whole scene was a funeral procession ready to take the dead to the cemetary. When the young friend tried to go on his way, the procession also went on, so he found himself in the crowd still. After a hundred yards or so, he managed to extricate himself and reached the cottage of the patient's father.

Three days later, the young porter died, and his friend noticed uneasily that the crowd and coffin were exactly the same as he had seen three nights before.

THE LEGEND OF ROCH CASTLE, Pembrokeshire

The gaunt tower of Roch Castle, rising from a mass of volcanic rock, is a landmark of many miles around St. Bride's Bay. This is the furthest north that the Normans pushed on the west coast of Pembrokeshire and the castle marks the boundary line between Welsh in the north and English to the south.

In the 13th century, the feudal Norman Lord, Adam de la Roche, had a premonition that he would die from an adder's sting. But he would not have to fear after a year had passed in safety. So he built the castle and esconced himself in the top storey. The year passed, and, with only a few days to go, everyone was rejoicing. But the wind blew across St. Bride's Bay and the wintry weather was bitterly cold. A servant brought in some firewood so the Lord of Roch could warm himself. He did so, but when he fell asleep before the embers, an adder crept from the remaining faggots of wood and stung him. In the morning, they found him dead.

ST. DAVID'S, Pembrokeshire

The most saintly figure in Welsh mythology is undoubtedly St. David. The first legend arose thirty years before his birth when St. Patrick, possible a Pembrokeshire man himself, came to St. David's and to the place where the Cathedral now stands, saw that it was a pleasant spot and vowed to serve God there. He was a little put out by a heavenly vision which told him the place was reserved for another not to be born for thirty years. So he went down to Whitesands Bay and turned his eyes to Ireland.

David's mother, St. Non, twice caused, by her very presence in pregnancy, a local holy man to cease preaching. Then during the saint's birth on the cliff-top, in a terrible storm of thunder and lightning, a stone on

which she leaned split in sympathy and the imprints of her hands were left on the stone. After curing the blindness of his master Paulinus, St. David was sent for to help preach, at Llandewi Brevi, against the Pelagian heresy. It was in fact a preaching contest for the title of archbishop. But nobody could make his voice heard by those furthest away. So Paulinus sent for David who, restoring a dead boy to life on the way, came to preach. A white dove descended, the ground rose beneath his feet, "he raised his voice until it rang like a trumpet. The heresy is expelled, the faith confirmed in sound hearts, thanks are rendered to God and St. David."

David's encounter with the nearby Irish chieftain Boia shows him at his most formidable. Boia was angry at the smoke rising from the holy men's settlement and encouraged by his wife, set out with his men to kill the monks. They were stricken with a fever and could only curse the monks. But their cattle were also struck down so Boia said to David: "The land shall be yours for ever." "Your cattle shall come to life again," replied the man of God kindly. But Boia's wife, evidently a forerunner of Lady Macbeth, afire with jealous spite, "called her maids and said 'Go where the monks can see you and with bodies bare play games and use lewd words'. The maids obeyed, and they played immodest games, imitating sexual intercourse and displaying love's seductive embraces. The minds of some of the monks they entice away to lust, the minds of others they irritate." Thus the words of Rhigyfarch, St. David's biographer. Some of the monks then wanted to leave the place; but the holy father stood firm: "We must stand fast; it is Boia who must give way," he said.

The next day, Boia's wife took her step-daughter, dressed her hair and cut off her head. A healing spring issued forth. Boia was killed by an Irish pirate Lysgi (Porthlysgi close by). Then, says Rhigyfarch, the monastery was built and, such was the austerity of the holy father that every monk toiled at daily labour and spent his life working with his hands. The monks ploughed themselves, not with oxen, and they dug the ground unwearily with hoes and mattocks. David was determined to keep the shoulders of the monks bowed down with pious labours for "Leisurely repose develops a spirit of instability and apathy with restless promptings to lust." The holy father kept them hard at it and "they do not serve course of different savours, nor richer kinds of foods; their food is, in fact, bread and herbs seasoned with salt." Not, as Rhigyfarch assured us, "to excess, for too much though it be of bread alone engenders self-indulgence."

A DEATH OMEN IN ST. BRIDE'S BAY, Pembrokeshire

The Tolaeth was a sound heard before a death. It was a rapping or knocking; sometimes thuds or shuffling. It was very widespread all over Wales and many people living today can vouch for it. Carpenters, for example, or their families, have heard knocking in the workshop as of their making a coffin – before a death.

A fisherman living on the shores of St. Bride's Bay was disturbed for three successive nights by sounds downstairs of shuffling feet, doors opening, and the noise as if men were carrying a burden and putting it down. His wife heard the same noises and they heard them only in the kitchen. Both were frightened because this could only be the Tolaeth.

A few weeks later their son was drowned and his body was brought home on a ladder. To their horror the sounds were reproduced exactly: the shuffling of feet, moving of chairs and the grunting sound of the men setting down their burden.

THE BRYNBERIAN AFANC'S GRAVE, Pembrokeshire

As you approach the village of Brynberian just off the B4329 from Cardigan to Haverfordwest over the mountain, the Preseli mountains lie on your left. About a quarter of a mile on your left across the moor is the Bedd yr Afanc (The Monster's Grave).

Little seems to be known of the Brynberian afanc except that he was caught in a pool near Brynberian Bridge and taken up and buried on the mountain-side.

The archaeologists say this is a Neolithic gallery grave from about 2500 B.C. and with an outer parallel row of stones on each side similar to those of southern Ireland.

ST. EDREN'S CHURCHYARD, Pembrokeshire

The ancient well in the churchyard of St. Edren's (B4330 from Haverfordwest to Croesgoch as far as Newton Cross and straight on) was a holy well. It cured madness but the ritual attached to it no longer exists.

According to tradition, the well dried up because of pollution: a woman washed clothes in it on a Sunday. Another tradition was that a farmer brought a mad dog to drink out of it, whereupon the farmer died but the dog recovered. Anyway, the virtue of the water was miraculously transferred to the grass growing round the base of the church walls, called 'porfa'r cynddeiriog', the grass of the mad. It was a cure for hydrophobia, and eaten as a sandwich between bread. A money offering was put in a stone trough in the church wall.

A Gwiber (flying snake) is said to have flown from St. Edren's church tower to near Grinston where it lives in marshy ground, at night time coiling up in the bottom of Grinston well. But it can hardly have flown from the present church which is entirely Victorian.

SIR RHYS AND THE KING AT DALE, Pembrokeshire

When the Earl of Richmond was about to land in Wales from France, Sir Rhys ap Thomas consulted a noted Wise Man in Dale to find whether the Earl would be successful in his bid to dethrone King Richard III. The wise man was reluctant to prognosticate but finally he did produce a cryptic rhyme:

> "Full well I wend, that in the end
> Richmond, sprung from British race,
> From out this land, the boare shall chase."

Henry VII, as the Earl of Richmond later became at Bosworth, needed some re-assurance too, after the landing, and he also went to a wise man Dafydd Llwyd, a bard and prophet. He was in doubt as well, but in his case it was resolved by his wife who advised him to prophesy in favour of Henry, since if the latter failed, Llwyd would hear no more about it, but if Henry won it would make his fortune.

Henry VII, the first Welsh king of England, landed from Brittany on 1 August 1485 at Mill Bay near St. Ann's Head.

His arrival placed Sir Rhys, the great potentate of south-west Wales, 'little less than a prince', in something of a moral quandary. He supported Henry strongly as a loyal Welshman, but he had given an oath of allegiance to Richard III, that he would permit no landing except over his body. Advised by the Bishop of St. David's that this was not binding, he brought his 8000 men to march with Henry but took the precaution of lying beneath Mullock Bridge to let the future Henry VII walk over his body.

PEMBROKE

An historical tale that has found its way into history books throughout the ages tells how Gerald of Windsor foiled the Welsh.

In the reign of Henry I, Arnulph de Montgomery erected 'a slender fortress with stakes and turf' which he consigned to his constable and lieutenant-general, Gerald of Windsor.

Giraldus Cambrensis relates how the Welsh were successfully besieging the Normans and the garrison was at its last gasp when Gerald had four hogs slaughtered and cut up and thrown down to the attackers. The stratagem was designed of course to show that they had plenty of food; and the following day he devised a more refined stratagem. He arranged that a letter written and sealed by him should be found at the house of Wilfred, Bishop of St. David's, who was visiting the area. The letter was to Arnulph and said there would be no need of any reinforcement for the next four months. This succeeded and the besiegers gave up and went home.

THE TREFGARN PROPHECY, Pembrokeshire

In the late eighteenth century, a farmer named Thomas Evans lived on a small farm named Penyfedr, near Trefgarn Rocks. Both Mr. Evans and his wife Sarah, were renowned for their piety. Mrs. Evans, a Bevan from

Martel Mill, was renowned possibly more for her ability to foresee future events.

Coming into the house one day, she said she had just seen a most remarkable sight in Trefgarn Valley below the house. She described it as a large number of heavily laden carts or wagons going very fast one after another, but with no bullock or horse pulling them; but the first one appeared, from the smoke she saw, to be on fire.

This was some fifty years before George Stephenson first introduced steam locomotive power. About 1850 the railway was brought to Pembrokeshire. The famous engineer Isambard Brunel intended to extend it northward towards Fishguard and cuttings were made in Trefgarn Valley so it was thought the prophecy would be fulfilled.

But Brunel abandoned the scheme and took the line to new Milford (now Neyland) instead. So strangely the prophecy seemed to be contradicted. And even when the branch line was later made, it was miles to the north of Trefgarn, so once again the old lady's prophecy was ridiculed.

But then it was found later by the G.W.R. that the old loop line via Letterston was not suitable for a fast direct service to London through Trefgarn Valley, Brunel's original idea, as foreseen by Mrs. Sarah Evans, and this is where the line now runs.

WITCHCRAFT AT MATHRY, Pembrokeshire

At Mathry there was a celebrated witch who people believed was guilty of often bewitching cattle. One day, when a servant girl of a farm in the neighbourhood went out to milk in the morning, she found all the cows in a sitting position 'like cats before a fire.' And whatever she did, she could not get them to move. The farmer suspected the witch so he went and made her come with him.

When she came, she said there was nothing wrong with the cows and she simply put her hand on the back of each animal and it immediately got up.

A PHANTOM FUNERAL AT PENALLY, Pembrokeshire

In the south of the county, the phantom funeral was known as a 'fetch funeral', and this account of one dates from mid-Victorian times.

A man working for the Vicar of Penally told him that on the previous evening he had met a large funeral procession near Holloway Farm, naming several neighbours among the mourners. The Vicar gently ridiculed the idea.

"But," said the man, "Curious thing was that they carried the coffin over a bank."

"Then surely," said the Vicar, "You can show me the place, since the hedge will be all trampled down."

The man pointed out a place in a narrow lane near Holloway Farm, assuring the Vicar that that was where the procession left the road and passed into a field. But when they looked there were no signs of any passage through the hedge.

Shortly after, Mr. Williams, the tenant of Holloway, died and as a snow-drift blocked the lane, the coffin was taken over the bank on the way to Penally cemetary.

THE MERMAN OF CASTLEMARTIN, Pembrokeshire

In her *Tour to Milford Haven*, published in 1791, Mrs. Morgan, related the following story.

A farmer, Henry Reynolds, of Pennyholt, went down one morning to the cliffs marking the boundary of his land. At the eastern end of a little bay by Linney Stack, he saw someone appearing above the water. He was a bit surprised since he knew it to be deep. He went nearer and was about ten yards off; it was a youth of 16 to 18, with a very pale skin.

The water was very calm and clear and there was no wind. The unknown youth was sitting, apparently, on a brown substance but when he moved, Reynolds saw that this was part of him and it was a long tail, like a conger eel. In deep water the tail went right down, and in shallow water it moved to the side. The youth swam around continually, in a circular motion. His body, above the waist at least, and his features were quite human he had rather short and thick arms and hands. From the forehead, a brownish substance more like ribbon than hair went up over his head and down his back into the water. The youth lifted it up at the back to wash underneath it.

The youth didn't grin or distort his face at all or make any noise, but his looks were wild and fierce. Reynolds stayed looking for an hour, but when he came back with others, the bay was empty.

BOSHERSTON & ST. GOVAN'S, Pembrokeshire

Close to Bosherston, that most attractive and unspoilt village, is St. Govan's Chapel. To get there, you go straight on from Bosherston until you get to the coast, and there, halfway down the cliff steps, is St. Govan's chapel and well.

The Ancient Monuments Commission Report says cautiously that the chapel 'may' be of 13th century construction, but St. Govan himself is unknown. He may have been, but a generation or two ago, people had no doubt but that he was Sir Gawaine; yet one more Arthurian figure linked with the county.

The pamphlet obtainable in the church gives a different origin for St. Govan.

The rock and well were protected by supernatural powers. Gawaine was hidden here by enchantment according to one story; escaping from pirates, says another. The rock opened letting him into a vertical cleft, then closed again, protecting him from his enemies. When they had gone, it opened again and it remains open, leaving the impression of his body. If anyone wishes in the cleft before turning round to come out, his wish will be fulfilled. The steps are said to be uncountable by mortals – different up and down (are there 52?), and whatever hopes are in one's mind when going up and down, if breathed lightly on the wind, will be granted.

Below are magic stones, which ring like bells when touched. In the arch above the chapel, a bell hung for centuries and often sounded without human aid. It was said that the sound of a bell was a death or a disaster at sea.

Just below the chapel under a stone hood is the holy well, and until this century it was visited by people with eye ailments and rheumatism. Earth from fissures round the chapel was sprinkled round farm and homestead to avert evil.

★ ★ ★

Another curious legend attached to St. Govan's: a farmer was sowing barley on Trevalen Down above St. Govan's, when he noticed a dignified, striking-looking stranger watching. The farmer approached him and in reply to the stranger's question, "What are you doing?" replied that he was "sowing barley." "But," said the stranger, "this seed you are putting into the ground will decay."

"Yes," said the farmer, "and it will spring again and at harvest time I shall gather it."

"Do you believe," asked the stranger, "that that which is dead can come to life?"

"I do," said the farmer.

"Then, go home," said the stranger quietly, "and get thy sickle and cut thy corn. For I am the Resurrection and the Life." The farmer did so, and on his return, the stranger had disappeared but the barley was ripe for harvesting the same day it had been sown.

Nearby on the cliffs is the Huntsman's Leap, where a lone rider leaped the chasm. Perhaps he died of fright on looking back, or perhaps he only accomplished the feat because his horse was blessed and he thus escaped losing the soul he had sold to the devil.

Bosherston Mere was frequented by apparitions and mysterious moans and wailings.

> There is nothing to hope and nothing to fear
> When the wind sounds low on Bosherston Mere
> There is much fear and little to hope
> When unseen hands pull St. Govan's rope;
> And the magic stones, as the wise know well,
> Promise sorrow and death, like St. Govan's bell.

The handsome farm buildings on the cross-roads leading to Bosherston are Sampson Farm which has one of three celebrated standing stones. The others are at Stackpole Farm and on Stackpole Warren and are said to meet annually "to dance the hay at Sais's (Saxon's) Ford, and then, the dance over, to resume their station."

It was said to be very good luck to see the dance, but on the other hand the devil played his flute and witches held their revels there.

THE WISTON BASILISK, Pembrokeshire

Long ago there were several claimants to the estate of Wiston, Castell Gwys, near Haverfordwest, which was founded by Wizo, the Flemish

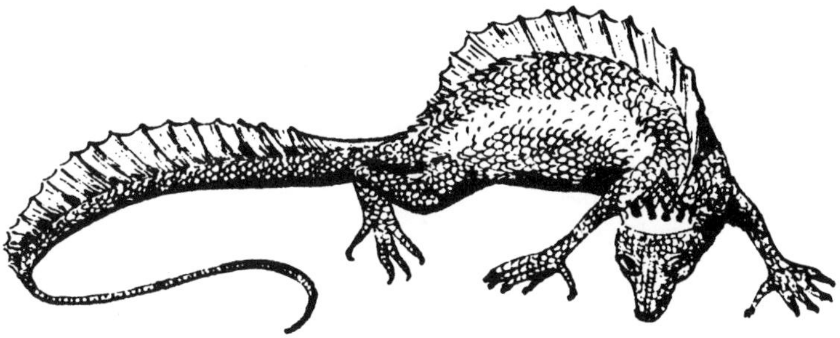

Lord of Dungleddy (Daugleddau), the area between the Western and Eastern Cleddau rivers.

A basilisk lived in a hide on Wiston Bank nearby, much feared by everyone; and rightly so, for the basilisk, though quite small – about a foot or two long, was a fabulous monster, a reptile with a black and yellow skin, death-dealing breath and eyes in the back its head as well as the front and the ability to kill by its baleful gaze. The only compensation was that if a human being saw the basilisk without being seen, the monster would die.

It was agreed that anyone who could look at the basilisk without being seen should inherit the estate. This seemed quite reasonable as anyone who was first seen by the monster would not live to inherit anyway. Several claimants tried unsuccessfully, until one thought of an idea. He took a barrel to the top of the hill and got inside. The he let it roll down the hill past the spot where the serpent lived. As he passed he looked through the bung and called out, "Ha, bold basilisk. I can see you but you can't see me." In this way, he became owner of the Wiston estates.

ST. BRIDE'S CHAPEL, Pembrokeshire

In the little bay of St. Bride's was once a great herring fishery; and just above the beach was once a small chapel where the fishermen used to pray both for success and that they might avoid the perils of the sea. According to Fenton, the Pembrokeshire historian. The stone coffins projecting today from the earth eroded by the sea at high water are those of fishermen. The chapel fell into disuse, and there is a tradition that out of the ruins of the chapel a salting house was made for the fish; but from that day the herrings failed. "When St. Bride's Chapel a salt-house was made St. Bride's lost the herring trade."

THE GWAUN VALLEY, Pembrokeshire

During the early part of last century, and later, the Gwaun Valley was reputedly full of witches, especially of the descendants of one particular old woman. One well-known family who practised the black art wanted to become members of Caersalem Baptist Chapel, and were admitted. But it made no difference to their behaviour.

One witch, even on the day she became a communicant, bewitched a young servant girl of Gelli Fawr farm. She was sitting in a pew behind the girl who rushed out of the chapel and ran wildly about the roads. Her father, having tried every means of pacifying her, went to Cwrt-y-Cadno to consult Dr. Harries, the famous Carmarthenshire Wise Man. Dr. Harries told the father what had happened and even showed him the scene in a mirror. He gave him a piece of paper with some words written on it which the girl had to wear on her breast. And this was quite sufficient to bring her back to a normal condition.

A WAKE NIGHT in the Gwaun Valley

An uncanny event took place at a Gwylnos (Wake-night) at Dolgarreg.

A notoriously ungodly old gentleman farmer had died and was laid out in his coffin. The candles were lit and the people came to the house. Wake-night went on as usual, according to the custom. Some of the lads and girls were making rather merry when there suddenly came a sound of horses galloping, approaching the house. The next moment the sound of men's footsteps was heard; the door opened and footsteps crossed the room where the Wake-night was being held; nothing was seen. But as they passed through, the invisible intruders put out the candles. Their presence could even be felt, but everyone was far too frightened to do anything. Then the footsteps left as they had come, the visitors re-lit the candles, the clatter of horses could be heard leaving and it gradually died away.

When the alarmed relatives and friends went into the room where the coffin was to see what had happened, there was nothing but an empty coffin; for the corpse was gone and it never was found. The coffin was afterwards filled with stones and buried.

A CORPSE CANDLE AT TENBY, Pembrokeshire

There is a tradition that St. David himself prayed that the people should have some sign to prepare themselves for death; and that there should also be a sign to the living of the reality of another world. In a vision he was told that the Welsh and apparently more particularly those in the St. David's diocese, would have some forewarning of when and where death might be expected. This takes the form of a Canwyll Corph, or Corpse Candle, and it is seen passing along the route of a funeral, or hovering round the spot the dead person would be, or where an accident would happen.

This particular story relates to a young mistress lodging near Tenby in a farmhouse.

One night she was lying awake when she saw a light like a little star moving towards her bed from the doorway. The light came to a standstill by her bed and lowered itself to her feet.

Terrified, she screamed and all the members of the household came running to find out what had happened, and then to comfort her.

Nothing more happened and some six weeks later she went off on holiday. While she was away, the farmer's wife, a strong healthy woman, was suddenly taken ill and quite unexpectedly died. The young schoolmistress was told and hurried back for the funeral. When she arrived and was taken upstairs she found that the body had been laid out in the spare bedroom she herself had occupied and where the light had appeared.

PENMAEN, Gower

On the wedding night of Rhys ap Iestyn at Pennard Castle, the sentries outside the gates heard the sound of unearthly music and then they saw a crowd of the Tylwyth Teg dancing in the moonlight. But when they told their Prince, Rhys was so drunk that he told them to drive the little people away and strike them down.

His wife was aghast at what might befall them if they did so, but Rhys would not listen to her.

"I fear no-one," he said boastfully.

But when he and his soldiers were outside, the little people had faded away. But a voice shouted out menacingly, "You shall suffer, Rhys; you have spoiled our innocent sport and your castle shall perish."

Then a terrible sandstorm blew up and the castle was slowly covered. Today the ruins remain, of the castle that was doomed three hundred years ago.

> "... the castle of Pennard, desolate and ruinous ... standeth on a rock near adjoining the sea, now encompassed with much sand ..."
>
> *Survey of Gower* 1650

LLANGENNITH, Gower

The name on the signposts is Llangennith but the Welsh name is Llangynnydd and it is pronounced locally as Llangenny. The name comes from St. Cennydd, a 6th century Celtic Saint.

As a small baby, he was taken badly crippled in one leg, to King Arthur's court, a child of the sin of incest. Because of the king's clemency, he was not put to death, but placed in a wicker basket which the currents of the Loughor River took to sea. But before the child could perish, gulls carried him on to Worms Head. There he lived, suckled at first by the brazen breast of the Titty Bell, providentially left there and later by a deer.

After eighteen years, he was given a sign to go and build a cell on Burry Holms, where he would find a spring.

More historically he is believed to have been a member of the college of Cattwg and he then founded the Cor Cennydd, a religious group at Llangennith. His legendary beginnings are commemorated in the wooden carvings in the lych-gate of the church. This is a 'clas' church, a monastery or important church, but much restored. Llanmadog, close by, was founded by St. Madog, a pupil of St. Cennydd.

ELIDORUS, in Gower

This story was told by Giraldus in his *Itinerary Through Wales*. It happened in the Gower neighbourhood. When Elidorus was a boy of 12 he ran away from school to avoid the strict discipline and frequent canings. He hid in a river bank where he found a hollow; after a couple of days he was getting pretty hungry and wondering what to do about it, when two little men came up to him and invited him to a country 'full of delights and sports'. He followed them with alacrity through a dark path and then out into a most attractive countryside with rivers, meadows, woods and fields.

He was taken to the king who questioned him at length and then handed him over to his son, who was about the same age as Elidorus. They played together, and Elidorus learned quite a bit of the language.

He often went back to his own world; sometimes by the way he had first come, and sometimes by a different way.

He described the little people to his mother at great length. They were very small, he said, but well built, with a fair complexion and long hair over their shoulders like women. They had small horses and greyhounds. They lived on a milk diet, made up 'into messes' with saffron, but they ate no meat or fish. They never took an oath and detested lies. They had no form of public worship, being devoted only to truth and each time they came back from our upper world, presumably from the markets, they couldn't stop talking about our infidelities, inconstancy and ambition.

But Elidorus's mother spoilt it: she wanted a present and he had told her they often played with golden balls, so she told him to bring one back for her.

And so he did, but he was followed by two little men, and in his haste, he stumbled just as he reached home. They pounced on him, seized the ball and derided him contemptuously as they ran back. Terribly upset that they should feel like that about him because of his mother, he tried to go back and explain but, try as he would, he couldn't ever find the passage by the river bank.

He got over it at last, and went on to train for, and eventually, become a priest; when questioned late in life by the Bishop of St. David's, David II, Elidorus told him the story.

He had learned quite a lot of the language of the little people and, according to the Bishop, it conformed in many ways to the Greek language, some words being identical, notably those for salt and water.

This is the only reported case of an identified Fairy language. Many of the Fairy wives and Mermaids were reported as having spoken in Welsh.

THE CAVE IN NEATH VALLEY

At Craig y Ddinas near Pont Fechan at the top of the Neath Valley is the setting for the most famous Welsh cave tale.

A Welshman walking across London Bridge with a hazel stick in hand was accosted by an Englishman who asked him where he came from. The young Welshman was suspicious but the Englishman reassured him.

"Don't take it amiss; it will be to your benefit, for that stick in your hand grew where are hidden vast treasures. Lead me there and you can share the treasure."

At length the Welshman was persuaded to take the Wise Man, for such he was, with him and they went back. Under where the old hazel grew was a broad flat stone which covered the entrance to a huge cavern. In the middle of the passage was a bell, which the Wise Man earnestly advised the Welshman not to touch. Then reaching the lower part of the cave, they found thousands of armed warriors sleeping in a large circle, heads outward, their armour, shields and swords bright and ready beside them, ready to be donned immediately the bell sounded. And amidst them was one distinguished by his battle-axe and crown of gold. In the middle of the circle were two heaps of gold and silver. The Wise Man told the Welshman he could take as much as he could carry from either heap. The Wise Man took none.

"If you accidentally touch the bell," he said, "and a warrior wakes, he will ask 'Is it day?', and you must reply: 'No, sleep thou on'."

So they left the cave, and the Welshman loaded with gold did touch the bell and a warrior awoke, but being re-assured, he went back to sleep again.

"Now," said the Wise Man, "if you are prudent, you have enough for life; you can go back for more, but take care not to wake the warriors. You have seen Arthur and his warriors asleep, ready for the day when the

Black Eagle and the Golden Eagle are at war. They will then wake and destroy the enemies of the Cymry and will repossess the Island of Britain and re-establish their king and government at Caerleon."

But the Welshman, improvident, did go back for more and did, on returning overloaded with gold, touch the bell. But he was so terror-struck that he forgot to answer the warrior whereupon some of the warriors got up and took away the gold and beat him so unmercifully that, after they had thrown him out, he could barely walk. And he could never find the entrance again.

CWRT Y CADNO, CAIO, Carmarthenshire

The greatest Dyn Hysbys, Wise Man, Seer or Wizard of modern times was Dr. John Harries of Cwrt y Cadno, Caio, Carmarthenshire. He died in 1835 and his son, also a wizard died in 1862. They were astrologers, healers, could discover missing people or objects and could overcome witchcraft.

Many accounts were told of Dr. Harries foretelling the future, or finding lost or stolen cattle. It was believed that the Harrieses could mark out thieves and those who had the 'Evil Eye'.

A Carmarthenshire man went to Harries, Cwrt y Cadno, to ask him where to find three lost cattle. The seer told him to come back the day after as he wanted to consult his books. The farmer, disappointed, went out and decided to sleep in the barn, without telling Dr. Harries. In the middle of the night, he awoke to see Dr. Harries in the barn summoning spirits before him. He then asked them where the cattle were. Eventually one spirit said they would be on Carmarthen Bridge at midday following. Next day the farmer went there, and there they were. He drove them away but soon they all fell down as if dead. Sadly he went back to Dr. Harries who said: "Serve you right. I put a spell on them because you left without paying me." So he paid and went back and the cattle were healthy again, and he drove them home.

LLYN-Y-FAN FACH, Myddfai, Carmarthenshire

A farmer who had died fighting for Welsh freedom at the end of the 12th century left a widow who then farmed at Blaensawdde near Llanddeusant. In time, her stock increased and she had to graze the cattle on the Black Mountains where their favourite place was near the little lake Llyn-y-Fan Fach.

Her son used to go and look after the cattle; to his amazement one day he saw a beautiful young lady sitting on the smooth surface of the water, combing her long hair. She saw the young man, who offered her some barley bread and cheese. She refused and gently evaded him, saying:

Cras dy fara	Hard baked is thy bread
Nid hawdd fy nala	It is not easy to catch me

and she dived under the water and disappeared.

He realised he had immediately fallen in love with her and when he got home, he told his mother. She advised him to take some unbaked bread the next day; which he did.

He waited for hours the next day but at last she came but she refused his offer saying:

Llaith dy fara	Unbaked is thy bread
Ti ni fynna	I will not have thee

But she smiled at him as she disappeared, so he took heart. His mother suggested taking some slightly better baked bread next day. He waited all day and as he was about to return, he saw some cows on the surface of the lake; and then the lady. This time she accepted his bread and after some persuasion she consented to become his wife but she would live with him only till she received from him three blows without a cause. He willingly agreed.

Then she returned to the lake coming back with another girl like her and a noble-looking old man who was her father. He told the young farmer he consented provided he could distinguish the girl he had chosen from her

sister. This he did only because she moved her foot slightly and he noticed a slight variation in the way she did up her sandals.

"You have chosen correctly," said he father, "be kind to her and I will give her as a dowry as many sheep, cattle, goats and horses as she can count without drawing breath." She immediately counted as rapidly as she could, counting in fives. And the animals came out of the lake when her father called them.

So they were married and lived happily for some years at Esgair Laethdy near Myddfai, and had three sons. But there was once a christening which the wife was reluctant to go to; and her husband touched her on the shoulder when she hadn't gone to fetch the horse; and she reminded him that this was the first blow.

Then, at a wedding, she burst into tears saying: "People are entering into trouble." And he touched a second time on the shoulder. Then after years had gone by, the third blow was struck. It was at a funeral where she appeared cheerful: "Because people, when they die, go out of trouble," and her husband reproved her with a touch. She went back to the lake, calling the animals by name, down to the "little black calf though suspended on the hook." Back they all went to the lake, the ploughing oxen leaving a great furrow behind them. The mother appeared to her sons at intervals and advised them on healing. They became the famous Physicians of Myddfai and became doctors to Lord Rhys Gryg of Llandovery and Dynevor. There have been numerous descendants who were doctors, the last dying in Aberystwyth about a hundred years ago.

In years gone by, the custom of going to the lake on the first Sunday in August was well established and thousands would go.

A further legend says that the disconsolate husband tried to drain the lake after his wife went, and a huge hairy monster came out and threatened to drown the town of Brecon.

CARREG CENNEN, Carmarthenshire

The ruined castle of Carreg Cennen, a few miles from Llandeilo, stands majestically 900ft above the Cennen river, the most striking situation of any Welsh castle. Although Norman in origin, it was held in Henry II's time by the Lord Rhys and a legend relates to the 50 yard passage, cavern if you like, running down from the south.

It is that a young servant was killed getting water for the beleagured garrison of Lord Rhys from a spring in the cliff face, and the passage was then cut to assure the castle garrison's water supply in time of siege.

Another legend connects the place with the strange figure of Owain Lawgoch. Along the bank of the river is Ogof Dinas, Castle Cave. Here, many years ago, a local farmer found a seated figure, cloaked, that of Owain Lawgoch.

Like Arthur he waits to be summoned to free Wales from the English. As a historical figure in the 14th century, he was called Ywain de Galles by the French. He claimed to be the heir of Llewelyn the Last, and King of Wales and fought cleverly for the French to the extent of preparing an invasion of Wales. Many Welshmen, recruited by the Black Prince to fight in the English armies in France – for they were the finest bowmen – deserted to Owain. Edward III was so alarmed that he decreed that no Welshman should command a castle in Wales. But then, an English spy, one John Lamb, whom Owain had saved and made his squire, cut his master's throat while performing his duty of cutting his hair.

Owain waits in many caves for the call to duty – Nant Gwynant in Caernarvon, in mid-Wales and several caves in the limestone rock round Llandybie and at Craig-y-Ddinas in Glamorgan. But according to an old Welsh ballad, he is not in a Welsh cave but 'tarries in a foreign land'. At Troed-yr-Aur near Newcastle Emlyn, the belief was that he slept somewhere in Wales near Offa's Dyke. And, at Ogo'r Ddinas, Llandybie, he and his men share the legend of Arthur and his followers.

REYNOLDSTON, Gower

The backbone of Gower is a ridge of Old Red Sandstone, Cefn Bryn which runs for 4 miles from Burry Green to Penmaen, and the rather straggling village of Reynoldston runs along the southern side of the middle part. Quite near where the road from north Gower crosses, stands the massive cromlech Coetan Arthur, Arthur's Stone. It is a Stone Age burial chamber about four thousand years old, with a 25 ton capstone.

It had some fame as a trysting place for local girls to test their lovers, but its more famous legend is that it was a pebble in Arthur's shoe which he removed and threw over his shoulder to fall on the common 7 miles away. Like the three famous stones in south Pembrokeshire which met annually for a dance, Coetan Arthur went down to the sea to drink on New Year's Eve.

LLANDYBIE

Llyn Llech Owen is a small lake forming the source of the Gwendraeth Fawr, on Mynydd Mawr. Once there was a man named Owen living on Mynydd Mawr who had a well (ffynnon) over which he kept a large flagstone which he was always careful to replace after he had taken enough water for himself or his horse. But one day he forgot to replace it after his horse had drunk, and then, looking back, was surprised to see that the well had burst out and was overflowing over a wide area. He galloped back and it was his horse's track in galloping round the water that limited its flow. It was believed that had he not returned, the well would have inundated the area.

In some places, the Owen was supposed to be Owain Glyndwr and also Owain Lawgoch who was highly esteemed in the folk-lore of the area. He and his men lived in a cave on Mynydd Mawr and, while there, used to water their horses at the well, which was covered by a flagstone needing a giant's strength to lift it. One day he forgot to replace it and the inundation took place. He went and told his men and they promptly fell into a deep sleep which is to last till the sound of a trumpet and the sound of arms when they will emerge to do battle.

Just a mile to the north of Llandybie in Carmarthenshire is a remarkable limestone hill; it is on a farm Cil yr Ichen. It is steep and high and on the top is the mouth of a very long cave. This is Ogo'r Ddinas, the cave of the fortress. There are many smaller caves leading out of it.

A story similar to that of Arthur in Craig y Ddinas is told. A certain Dafydd Meurig of Bettws Bledrws quarrelled with his father and set out for England going as a cattle drover, and on the way he cut a hazel stick. On London Bridge he was accosted by a stranger, and after the latter assuring him that there were wonderful things under the tree the stick had grown on, they returned.

They reached the spot and dug a little whereupon they found a great hollow place underneath. At the bottom of the stairs, they found a great table at the head of which sat a huge man about seven feet tall, his head on his left hand, asleep. In his right hand he grasped a long sword, and at his feet lay a big dog. The wizard said to Dafydd: "This is Owain Lawgoch, who is sleeping until it is time to awake and reign over the Britons." Around them they saw arms and gold bearing the images of different kings of Britain. They visited the cave several times, but then Dafydd could never find it again.

RHYS PRICHARD'S GOAT

The Reverend Rhys Prichard (1579-1644), Vicar of Llandovery, was one of the great Welsh churchmen of his time. Crowds came to hear him preach and when they were too great for his church, he preached in churchyards and in the open fields. He was a strong Royalist and a Calvinist and firm believer in Predestination and the salvation of the Elect; and he was intolerant of Catholic and Puritan alike.

In his youth at Oxford he was more inclined to drinking than studying

for the Church, and when appointed Vicar of Llandovery, he was notorious for his drunkenness. He spent most of his time in taverns.

He had a large goat which he sometimes took with him and one day, out drinking, he offered it some ale. The goat liked the taste and both Vicar and goat drank till they were hopelessly intoxicated. The next time he went drinking, the goat went too, but when he offered it ale again, the animal recoiled in disgust. This affected the Vicar as nothing had done before.

"How much wiser than I am," he said to himself, "this poor animal can profit where I cannot."

And from that day on, he reformed and touched not a drop of drink again.

More than that, henceforth, the Vicar became a great preacher of the Gospel in west Wales. And he also wrote poems which were gathered together as 'Canwyll y Cymry', the Welshman's Candle, and which have made his name live for over three hundred years.

PANTANNAS, MERTHYR TYDFIL, Glamorgan

This is the classical tale of the Fairies' Revenge.

A good while ago there was a farmer at Pantannas who thoroughly disliked the Fairies, or the Bendith y Mamau, the Mothers' Blessing, as they were called in Glamorgan. This was particularly unfortunate as there were several fields on the farm which they liked so much that they were almost always there.

At last he was told by a witch how to get rid of the "noisy, boisterous and pernicious tribe," as he called them. All he had to do was to plough up the grassland they liked so much; this he did and he sowed wheat instead. The Fairies stopped coming immediately and the sound of their music was no longer heard.

One evening when he was returning home, the farmer was met by a small man in a red coat who said menacingly to him:

"Vengeance is coming

It is approaching soon."

Although the farmer made light of it, he was disturbed. Then, a few nights later, a voice repeated:

"Vengeance is coming."

Then one night, the corn crop was burnt up.

The next day, the farmer met the little man again.

"It's only beginning," said the fairy, menacingly.

The farmer, thoroughly scared, tried to placate the fairy but even though he promised to restore the meadows, the fairy said their vengeance would take place, whatever happened. After much pleading, the fairies relented and said that their revenge would not take place in the farmer's lifetime nor that of his children. In fact a century passed by and the Pantannas family almost became accustomed to an occasional voice threatening revenge.

But then one Christmas when the heir of Pantannas was celebrating his engagement to the daughter of the neighbouring farm, Pen Craig Daf, a piercing angry voice shrieked:

"The time for vengeance has come."

The voice came from the Black Cauldron pool in the River Taff.

That night, the heir of Pantannas escorted his fiancee back home and never returned to Pantannas. The parents hunted everywhere, but no trace could be found; it was assumed he had been lured into a fairy ring and taken to one of their caves. Then, years after, the parents died; years later, the fiancee died. All this while, the fairies too, had disappeared.

Then many years after, the heir re-appeared. He went to Pen Craig Daf but all were strangers there; then to Pantannas where equally, he knew nobody. The farmer there recalled a story of a youth disappearing many, many years before. He accidentally knocked his walking stick against the returned heir, who promptly vanished in a shower of dust.

LLYN SYFADDAN (Llangorse Lake), Brecon

Not far from Llansantffraid is Llangorse Lake which is the second largest natural lake in Wales, after Llyn Tegid. There is an artificial island (crannog) in the lake dating from the Iron Age, and a dug-out canoe from it is in Brecon Museum.

"A towne drowned by an earthquake," as Aubrey said in 1656, is only one of the legends about the lake.

From here comes the oldest of the persistent and widespread tales of the Fairy wife who leaves after having been hit or touched by iron. Walter Map's 12th century miscellany tells how Gwestin living beside Brechnock Mere saw women dancing in his field of oats on three moonlight nights and he followed them until they sank in the water. He heard them saying to each other: "Had he done so-and-so he would caught one of us."

So, on the fourth night, he did; and he caught one who willingly became his wife but said she would serve him only till he should strike her with his bridle.

After presenting him with numerous children, she was accidentally struck with the iron of his bridle and ran away with the children. Gwestin chased her and with difficulty caught his son Trinio.

The latter disappeared after a battle with the men of Brychan of Brycheiniog, who died about the middle of the 5th century. People believed Trinio was not dead but had been rescued by his mother and taken back to the lake.

When the country was being oppressed by Henry I, the ancient saying that only a 'natural prince of the country' could command all the birds to sing, was proved by Gryffydd Rees much to the consternation of his Norman associates and the King, who put a price on his head. Giraldus also tells that the inhabitants sometimes saw the lake "covered and adorned with buildings, pastures, gardens and orchards." (Giraldus too was writing in the 12th century.) Even at the end of the 19th century, there was still a legend of a lost inundated city whose church bells could be heard in rough weather.

But there is also a retribution legend: once the town and all the land round belonged to a princess who had an admirer she would not marry until he had procured plenty of gold. So he one day murdered and robbed a man with much gold. The princess married him without delay but was worried about reports that the dead man's ghost was haunting the place where he had been murdered.

When the murderer was waiting to lay the ghost, he heard a voice say: "Should not innocent blood be avenged?" And another voice replied: "Not until the ninth generation."

So the princess felt safe, they had children and the town prospered and became more wicked. The princess and her husband lived to see the ninth generation and then, when they were celebrating, they were all drowned by a tremendous cataclysm which produced the present lake.

On linguistic grounds, Sir John Rees suggests that this legend stems from the times when the Goidels (Irish) ruled the area, i.e. in the post-Roman times. Irish invaders ruled much of north and most of west Wales for centuries.

LLANFABON, Glamorgan

Like the tale of Pantannas, the Llanfabon changeling story shows the Fairies as rather unpleasant. Perhaps the south Wales 'Bendith y Mamau' were less sociable than the Tylwyth of north Wales. But then, the human reaction towards them seems to have been less pleasant. For example, there are tales of the Fairies being left a bowl of urine instead of milk, a practice which, not unnaturally, infuriated them.

At one time Llanfabon was full of Bendith y Mamau. They kept the village awake all night with their music; they were very ugly and noisy too.

At Berth Gron farm lived a young widow, and she had to put up with a lot from the Bendith. Finally her baby boy was stolen and an ugly changeling left in his place. She kept him for a year and he didn't grow, so she went to a Wise Man and asked for advice on how to get her own back.

She was told to break an egg and mix it well in half the shell, taking care the changeling saw. She reported back that the changeling had said:

"An acorn was before the oak, and the oak is in the earth, but never before have I seen anyone make a pasty for the reapers in an egg-shell."

"Oh yes," said the Wise Man "He's of the old breed."

Then he told her to go to a nearby ford and hide. This she did, and saw a great crowd of the Bendith, with their music and in the midst her son. The Wise Man had told her to do nothing then, and she went home. Afterwards, she had to take a black hen and bake it whole. This she did, and then she fainted. When she came to, the changeling had gone, but her son was back.

GENILLYN THE THIEF, Glamorgan

Genillyn from north Wales asked for shelter at the house of Traer in south Wales; he was carrying a bridle round his neck and spurs at his belt.

After a frugal supper he sat silent; then he said to Traer: "You are wondering who I am and what I am doing. I have come because of the fame of a mare owned by a man in these parts and he guards her with such care that for a month all my ambushes have been in vain."

Traer said, "You in the north are certainly slow and cowardly by our standards. We would have made an attempt to get her and even have died rather than hang about a whole month. Tell me where she is and wait here three days with my wife and children and see how I do."

Said Genillyn, "We know all about the boasting of your people. Cadwallon, the son of Uther, has the mare at Gelligaer. She feeds by day in the midst of his soldiers. At night she is on a fine carpet (brachen) in the far corner of his house, with the whole household between her and the only door and four of his best men between her and the fire. You shall get ten cows for the mare and five for the carpet." Traer strolled up unconcernedly, as no thief in Wales is arrested but killed on the spot, and checked that the facts were right.

The first night was dark and starless. With his knife he made a hole beside the door and let himself in. He stole up to the mare and loosed her. Then out of sheer high spirits he tied the fringes of the carpet to her tail. The four men were sleeping on the carpet and the mare dragged them bodily through the fire which, covered with ashes, was outside the door. The whole band set out after him guided by the sparks. These he quenched and got back home safely; handed over the mare, received the cows and gained for himself great renown for daring as against the men of the north.

SHEE WELL, Glamorgan

This is also called Ogmore Spring, near the western boundary of St. Bride's Major, to the south-west of Ewenny. Three springs met there and water-ogres lived at their source and they captured and imprisoned girls. One who did get away became dumb so she could not tell about her experiences.

A time came when the Well dried up; it groaned and moaned and toads and snakes instead of fish were found in the Ogmore and Ewenny rivers; this was because the Well was offended by some evil men, living on the banks of the rivers. The Well receded to a cavern in the hills and to this the, by now, penitent wicked men went and promised to reform if the Well ogre relented and caused the Well to return to normal. The ogre agreed and even improved the whole place by planting trees.

LLANTONY

It was at Llantony Abbey that Giraldus Cambrensis tells a story about King Richard and the monastic orders, which were then great and powerful in influence and even more in possessions.

Fulke, a good and holy man, said to the King: "You have three daughters namely, Pride, Luxury and Avarice; and as long as they shall remain with you, you can never expect to be in favour with God." To which the King, after a short pause, replied: "I have already given away those three daughters: Pride to the Templars, Luxury to the Black Monks and Avarice to the White."

Another version, attributed to the historian Holinshed makes the King say "My covetousness I bequeathe to the Cistercians, for they covet the devil and all; and my lechery I commit to the prelates of the church who have most pleasure and felicitie therein."

It was a common complaint that the Cistercians were none too particular how they acquired the huge areas of land on which they had their enormous flocks of sheep. Giraldus had no particular liking for the Monastic orders but he was a prelate of the church himself so perhaps he thought the last part of the royal remark was a bit too near the knuckle.

THE DOVEY: THE BIRTH OF TALIESIN, Merionethshire

This was in the time of the Cantre'r Gwaelod, the land in Cardigan Bay, drowned according to the legends around 500 A.D. The district had been divided between two chiefs, Seithenyn and Gwyddno. The children of the latter had adopted a religious life; younger sons for whom there was no future, went into the Church; only it wasn't really a Church in those days. So they became monks.

Elfin, Gwyddno's son, was a disciple of Illtyd. He had a fishing weir on the sands between the Dovey and Aberystwyth, which brought in considerable wealth annually. But Elfin was an unlucky man and nothing of his prospered. His father gave him the weir for one more year. One morning Elfin visited the weir and found nothing but a leather bag fastened to one of the piers. His companion reproached him for the lack of fish – it ought to have produced a £100 on May eve.

"Anyway," said Elfin "perhaps there's a £100 worth in the bag." But in the bag was only a child.

"What a noble forehead," said Elfin's companion.

"Let his name be Taliesin 'noble forehead'," replied Elfin. And he took the baby home, where his wife nursed him carefully. And his wealth increased from that day.

Taliesin became one of Wales's most famous bards and poets.

Sources

The main historical sources are:

Giraldus Cambrensis. 'Itinerary through Wales' & the 'Description of Wales'. Translated Hoare, published Dent, Everyman 1908.

'The Mabinogion'. Trans. Guest, published T. Fisher Unwin, 1902.

Geoffrey of Monmouth's 'Historia Regum Britanniae', 12th century, widely known in the Middle Ages, and regarded by historians as highly unreliable.

Nennius' 'History of the Britons,' Ed. J. A. Giles. Published London 1910, Bell & Sons.

Walter Map 'De Nugis Curialium'. Translated M. R. James.

J. Rhys. 'Celtic Folklore', Oxford 1901.

Rev. J. Ceredig Davies: 'Folklore of Mid and west Wales' Aberystwyth 1991.

Rev. Elias Owen. 'Welsh Folklore' 1888. Republished E. P. Publishing Co. 1976.

T. Gwynn Jones, 'Welsh Folklore & Folk Custom', London 1930.

F. J. North, 'Sunken Cities' Cardiff 1957.

There are plenty of other books of Welsh Folk and Fairy tales, but only the above give the source of all tales; but of those that do not, the *Readers Digest Compendium of Folklore, Myths and Legends of Britain* is interesting. Apart from Giraldus and The Mabinogion, available in paperback, you will probably find it difficult to get any of the others.

Index

In a booklet of this size, it is not really possible to give enough space for a complete index. I have put in all geographical place-names and types of tale and even all the Saints mentioned; but, rather arbitrarily, the cast list of the Mabinogion tales has had to be omitted.